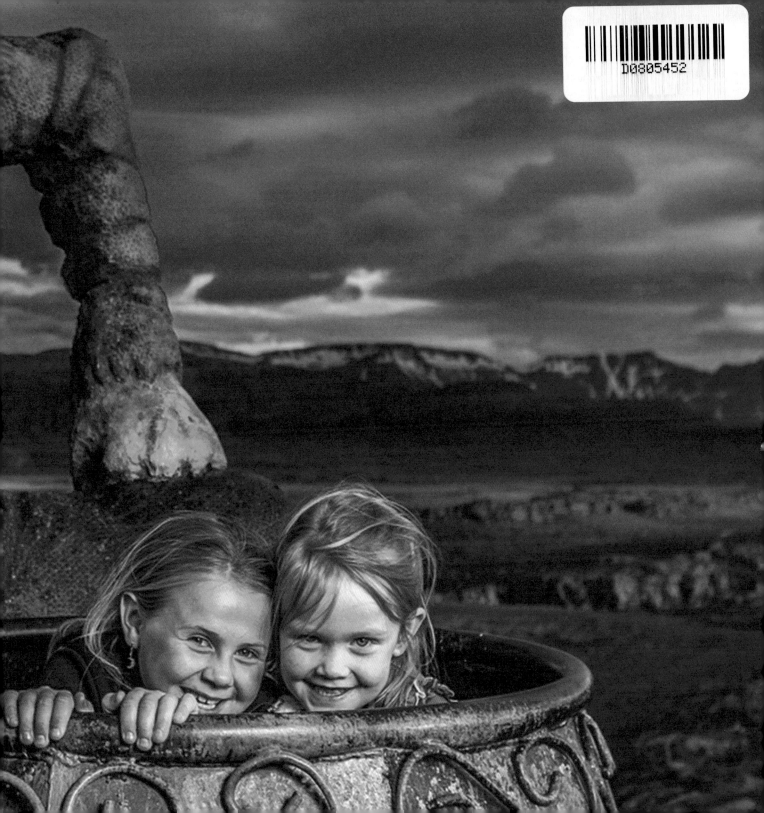

SCANDINAVIAN *classic* DESSERTS

PAT SINCLAIR

SCANDINAVIAN

classic

DESSERTS

Photography by Joel Butkowski

Foreword by Beatrice Ojakangas

PELICAN PUBLISHING COMPANY

GRETNA 2013

The word "Pelican" and the depiction of a pelican are trademarks of Pelican Publishing Company, Inc., and are registered in the U.S. Patent and Trademark Office.

ISBN: 9781455617463
E-book ISBN: 9781455617470

Recipes and Text by Pat Sinclair

Photography by Joel Butkowski

Design and Production by Sea Script Company

Layout based on a design by Kit Wohl

Endsheet photographs by Ragnar Th Sigurdsson/VisitIceland.com (front)
and Elina Sirparanta/VisitFinland.com (back)

Printed in China

Published by Pelican Publishing Company, Inc.

1000 Burmaster Street, Gretna, Louisiana 70053

CONTENTS

CAKES

PUDDINGS & CUSTARDS

TARTS & FRUIT DESSERTS

COOKIES & BARS

TRADITIONAL FAVORITES

FOREWORD

Traveling in Scandinavia and Finland is always inspirational. I snap mental pictures of linen covered tables spread with platters of buttery cookies, crispy pastries and a golden braided loaf. Coffee cups, a little larger than demitasses, set on saucers with little spoons nestled next to the cup and a pretty napkin pulled through the handles. This set-up is usual. The occasion can vary. Once, it was a birthday party at a friend's home. The table was set with seven different items, including a sweet bread (cardamom flavored), an un-iced cake, a fancy, filled cake and four varieties of little cookies and pastries. The protocol is set. With the first cup of coffee it was proper to sample a slice of cardamom bread and a cookie or small pastry. With the second cup of coffee, you sample a slice of the un-iced cake along with a cookie or pastry. With the third cup of coffee you sample the fancy, filled cake. It is not proper to dive into the fancy cake first nor to pile your plate high! On another occasion, I happened into a bank in Stockholm. It was the bank's anniversary and they were serving coffee, cardamom bread, and ginger cookies called "pepparkakor." In old Swedish, the word "peppar" was used for all spices, including cinnamon, nutmeg and cloves. The correct name for these cookies could be "spice cookies."

There is hardly a Nordic family that doesn't have a handful of favorite dessert recipes for cakes, cookies, tarts and holiday "must-haves." Until we visited Sweden, Norway and Denmark while researching my *Great Scandinavian Baking* book, my only real connection with Scandinavian cooking was the friendships I enjoy in Duluth. I knew that a Norwegian family would not serve coffee at Christmas without delicate Krumkake on the table, or a Swedish family couldn't imagine a holiday without crispy sugar-dusted Rosettes. Danes might make a feast of Aebelskiver hot from the pan. I just had to visit the "old country" to find out if this was true. It was.

Bakery browsing is one of my favorite activities when traveling. While others find every cathedral and museum, I never miss a patisserie or a Konditorei, making the choice impossible if I want something with my coffee. I just point out "one of this" and "one of that" and wrap what I can't eat in a napkin. I take careful notes and sketch out details. (My photography skills could be improved!)

On a trip to northern Sweden during Christmas Market Days, I was in the proverbial "pig heaven." Booths with homemade cakes, cookies and pastries lined the streets of Dalarna villages were there for the buying. I did my sampling along with tiny cupfuls of "Glögg," the sweet mulled wine so popular in Nordic countries.

At the beginning of Advent in Finland, piggy-shaped spice cookies signal that Christmas is coming. Hearts, stars, gingerbread boys and girls are traditional, too. I was curious about the use of animal shapes, not only in baked goods but also in Christmas decorations. I noted the "julbakka," a straw goat that almost every Swedish family had. Scholars believe this tradition goes back to pagan times, when animals were slaughtered to appease the gods and poor people substituted animal-shaped baked goods and straw decorations. After Christianity was introduced, the animal shapes were carried over in the form of cookies.

Scandinavian Classic Desserts is not just a cookbook of great recipes, but one that celebrates classics and "spin-offs" from old-time Scandinavian favorites. Enjoy your new book!

— Beatrice Ojakangas, Author of 29 cookbooks including *Great Scandinavian Baking Book*, Member James Beard Cookbook Hall of Fame (2005)

INTRODUCTION

SCANDINAVIAN HOSPITALITY, recognized all over the world, is a centuries-old tradition that started with the Vikings. The Viking god, Odin, dictated that a warm welcome should always be available to travelers, and that welcome continues today. Viking heritage, ancient customs and cuisines based on the land are an important part of the common heritage of all the Scandinavian countries. In addition to the extremes of the northern climate, rugged mountains, green forests and crystal clear lakes, all of these countries have long coastlines and seafaring traditions.

The countries most often considered Scandinavian are Sweden, Norway and Denmark, but Iceland and Finland are sometimes included because they are similar in many ways.

These countries are the northernmost countries in Europe and are somewhat isolated because of the position of the Scandinavian peninsula. Over the centuries, several of these countries have been united at various times. Sweden ruled Norway and Denmark for many years. Finland was ruled by Sweden and then Russia. This area of Europe is the least populated and most prosperous, and is filled with ancient castles, extraordinary scenery and soaring modern architecture in metropolitan areas.

These five Nordic countries have many breads, cookies and desserts in common. Their tarts are baked brimming with the intensely flavored berries and fruits that grow in the short summers. Celebrations such as "Midsommar" aren't complete without traditional foods and activities. The Christmas season is a season of lights and festivities to counter the darkness of the short northern days.

In Sweden, "fika" is the time when friends or family take a break and gather over coffee and sweet baked goods to visit and share news. More elaborate coffee tables always include an elegant dessert as a final course, often a whipped cream cake with fresh fruits. The American coffee break probably originated when Swedish immigrants gathered for coffee and visiting during a break in factory work.

Scandinavian Classic Desserts features national treasures like Swedish Princess Cake, Norwegian Blotkake and Danish Red Fruit Pudding. From elaborate cakes to homey puddings you'll find everyday desserts and the perfect endings to special celebrations. Favorites from MoMo's kitchen recall days of baking in warm kitchens filled with the fragrance of cardamom and buttery pastries and cakes.

Recipes are carefully written with attention to detail guaranteeing success. As with all baking, use high-quality ingredients such as unsalted butter and pure vanilla extract. Take the time to grind cardamom seeds to provide optimum flavor. Baker's Tips at the end of the recipes provide additional information to aid novice and experienced bakers alike. Bake something today and share it with someone you love.

—Pat Sinclair

Old Mill on Bornholm
Pia Britton VisitDenmark.com

Norwegian Fjord
Galyna Andrushko/Shutterstock.com

CAKES

DELICATE AIRY CAKES SMOTHERED IN WHIPPED CREAM are found everywhere in the Scandinavian countries. Fondness for these desserts is related to the richness of the dairy products from local farms and the concentrated flavors of berries and fruits that grow during the long hours of daylight in the brief northern summers.

You can prepare the sponge cake layers using a large bowl and wire whisk with lots of beating, but today's heavy-duty mixers make the process much less tiring. Hand mixers will work but require lengthening the beating times. For tender, airy results, beating sufficient air into the eggs is critical. Carefully fold ingredients by bringing your spatula across the bottom of the bowl and up the side in a circular motion enclosing the flour. Continue this motion until the flour is incorporated.

Cake flour has lower protein content and makes the most tender cakes, but all-purpose flour is an acceptable substitute. Just remove 2 tablespoons from each cup of all-purpose flour when replacing cake flour.

Have the cake ingredients at room temperature for the best results. The maximum amount of air can be beaten into whole eggs and egg whites when they are at room temperature. For the best results when whipping cream, chill the mixing bowl and beaters before beginning. Once the cream starts forming soft peaks, gradually add the sugar and vanilla and continue beating just until the sugar dissolves.

Any of the cakes in this chapter will make a perfect ending to a meal shared with family or friends. Swedish Berry Cream Cake, Strawberry Cream Cakeroll and Norwegian Blotkake are perennial favorites and taste best at the height of the season for fresh berries. Finnish Orange Cake and Frystkake are perfect with a cup of coffee. You'll be proud to serve any of these luscious cakes to your guests.

Finnish Orange Cake

Cardamom is the most popular spice in all of the Scandinavian countries. For the best flavor, buy the cardamom pods and grind the seeds as needed. Ground cardamom quickly loses it flavor.

SERVES 10 TO 12

1 1/2 cups	all-purpose flour		1 cup	sugar
1 teaspoon	ground cardamom		2 large	eggs
1/2 teaspoon	baking powder		3/4 cup	sour cream
1/2 teaspoon	baking soda		1 tablespoon	grated orange peel
1/4 teaspoon	salt		Whipped cream, if desired	
1/2 cup	unsalted butter, softened			

Heat the oven to 350°F and place the rack in the lower third of the oven. Spray a 9 x 5-inch loaf pan with nonstick cooking spray for baking, or grease the pan and lightly coat it with flour.

Combine the flour, cardamom, baking powder, baking soda and salt in a medium bowl.

Beat the butter in the bowl of a heavy-duty mixer on medium speed until creamy. Gradually add the sugar, scraping down the sides of the bowl occasionally, and beat until creamy. Beat 2 minutes.

Add the eggs, 1 at a time, beating after each addition and scraping down the sides of the bowl. Beat 3 minutes on medium or until the mixture is very light and creamy.

Reduce the mixer speed to low. Beat in half of the flour, the sour cream and the remaining flour, scraping down the sides of the bowl after each addition. Stir in the orange peel.

Pour the batter into the prepared pan. Bake 45 to 55 minutes or until golden brown and a toothpick inserted in the center comes out clean. Cool 10 minutes on a wire cooling rack. Loosen sides of cake from pan and invert the cake onto the rack. Place right side up and cool completely.

Serve with whipped cream, if desired.

Finnish Children Enjoying a Festival
VisitFinland.com

FINLAND

Finland has many similarities with the Scandinavian countries of Sweden, Norway and Denmark but isn't technically part of Scandinavia. From the Middle Ages to 1809, a period of over 600 years, Finland was actually a part of Sweden and still a has a large number of Swedish-speaking residents. During one of its many wars, Sweden lost Finland to Russia; Russian Czars ruled until the Russian Revolution in 1917. Much Swedish and Russian influence is still seen today. In 1917 Finland fought and won independence from Russia. After the Nazis and Russians became allies, Russia attempted to conquer Finland again, but during the Winter War, Finnish white-camouflaged ski troops fought them off. At the end of WWII, Finland landed in the Russian sphere of influence until the U.S.S.R. dissolved.

Sparsely populated, Finland is a land covered with forests and lakes, even in the capital of Helsinki. One third of Finland lies north of the Artic Circle, where the winter months are very cold and dark. But in the summer months of June and July in the extreme north, the sun doesn't set. Summers are short, but the days are warmed by the Gulf Stream.

Swedish Berry Cream Cake

Every Scandinavian country celebrates the arrival of spring berries by baking light airy cakes and smothering the layers in whipped cream and fresh berries. Whipped cream cakes accented with juicy berries are an important part of any summer celebration, especially "Midsommar," the celebration of the longest day of the year. Always grate the lemon peel before juicing the lemons.

Serves 6

Lemon Curd

1/2 cup	sugar		1/4 cup	cold unsalted butter, cut into 1/2 inch pieces
1/2 cup	freshly squeezed lemon juice		2 large	egg yolks, well beaten
			2 teaspoons	grated lemon peel

Cake

1 cup	cake flour		1 teaspoon	pure vanilla
1 teaspoon	baking powder		2 tablespoons	water
1/4 teaspoon	salt		1 cup	heavy whipping cream
5 large	eggs, room temperature		1 tablespoon	sugar
1 cup	sugar		1 teaspoon	vanilla
			3 cups	assorted berries

Make the lemon curd by combining the sugar, lemon juice, butter, egg yolks and lemon peel in a small heavy saucepan and cook over medium-low heat, stirring constantly. The butter will be just melted when the curd thickens. Bring the mixture just to the point where some bubbles rise and the sauce has thickened, 6 to 8 minutes. An instant read thermometer should read 185°F. Use a silicone spatula for stirring, and cook until sauce coats the spatula. When you draw your finger across the back of the spatula, the path should remain.

Strain into a small bowl. Cover surface with plastic wrap. Cool to room temperature and refrigerate several hours.

Heat the oven to 350°F and place the rack in the middle of the oven. Line the bottoms of 2 9-inch baking pans with parchment or waxed paper. Lightly spray liners with nonstick cooking spray.

Sift the cake flour, baking powder and salt together.

Beat the eggs, sugar and vanilla in the bowl of a heavy-duty electric mixer with the whisk attachment until thick and lemon colored, about 5 minutes. Gently fold in half of the flour mixture, the water and the remaining flour. Divide the batter into the prepared pans. Spread evenly.

Bake 20 to 22 minutes or until center springs back when lightly touched. Cool 10 minutes on wire cooling rack. Loosen sides of cake from pans and invert onto rack. Carefully peel off paper. Turn layers right side up and cool completely.

Beat the whipping cream in the bowl of a heavy-duty electric mixer with the whisk attachment until soft peaks form. Add the sugar and vanilla and continue beating until the sugar is dissolved.

Antique Tractor in Front of an Antique Barn
Conny Sjostrom/Shutterstock.com

Perfect Whipped Cream

Heavy whipping cream, also called whipping cream and heavy cream, contains 36% to 40% butterfat. Ultra-pasteurized whipping cream is processed to stay fresh longer but won't beat as high as whipping cream. One cup of heavy whipping cream equals 2 cups whipped cream.

The final use of the whipped cream affects how much you will want to beat it. When spooning it on top of a dessert or using as a garnish, beat until soft peaks form. If you want to pipe decoration using a pastry bag, the cream needs to be whipped until it holds its shape.

Whipping cream whips to the greatest volume when the cream is well chilled. Place the bowl and beaters in the freezer for about 30 minutes before using. Start beating on medium speed to prevent the cream from splashing out of the bowl. As the cream starts to thicken, you may increase the speed to high. For sweetened whipped cream, beat in 1 to 2 tablespoons sugar and 1 teaspoon vanilla.

Place 1 layer of the cake on a serving dish. Top with the lemon curd. Add the second layer and spread with the whipped cream. Garnish with fresh berries. This cake must be refrigerated because of the whipped cream and tastes best the day it is made.

Scandinavian Almond Cake

The first time I tasted this classic cake was at a Holiday Open House at my friend Carol's home. The cake immediately became a favorite of mine. You will need a special pan for this delicately flavored cake. The rounded ridges of the pan delineate the slices. Although a generous dusting of confectioners' sugar is all that is needed, I like to serve with sliced ripe peaches in the summer when they are in season.

SERVES 18

1 1/4 cups	all-purpose flour	1 1/2 teaspoons	pure almond extract
1/2 teaspoon	baking powder	2/3 cup	2% milk
1/4 teaspoon	salt	1/2 cup	unsalted butter, melted and cooled
1 cup	sugar		
1 large	egg, beaten		

Heat the oven to 350°F and place the rack in the middle of the oven. Spray a ridged 12-inch baking pan generously with nonstick cooking spray.

Combine the flour, baking powder and salt in a small bowl.

Whisk together the sugar, egg and almond extract in a medium bowl until light. Stir in the milk. Gently fold in the flour mixture until it disappears. Fold in the butter. Pour the batter into the prepared pan.

Bake 40 to 50 minutes or until the edges are golden brown and a toothpick inserted in center comes out clean. The edges of the cake will be starting to pull away from the sides of the pan. Place on wire cooling rack. Cool completely before removing from pan, at least 1 hour.

Serve with fresh fruit, if desired.

BAKER'S TIP: You can also top the cake with a thin glaze. Mix 1 cup confectioners' sugar and 1 to 2 tablespoons milk in a small bowl until smooth. Drizzle over cake allowing to drip down sides.

Escalators in the Stockholm Metro Station
Mikhail Markovskiy/Shutterstock.com

STOCKHOLM, SWEDEN

Stockholm, the capital of Sweden, is the largest and most populous urban area in Scandinavia. It is located on 14 islands at the mouth of Lake Malaren where it flows into the Baltic Sea. These islands are part of the Stockholm archipelago that extends eastward about 60 kilometers and contains over 24,000 islands. Stockholm is about one-third parks, one-third city and one-third water. The islands of the city are connected by bridges and to the east, north and south there are lakes and forests.

The city of Stockholm originally was centered in what is today called the old town or Gamla Stan, with buildings dating from the earliest days of the city. Stockholm was founded in 1252 and still features cobbled streets and medieval alleys. Because Sweden traded with Amsterdam, Talinn and Lubeck, its architecture reflects both Viking and Germanic influences.

Kungstradgarden, a royal city park, is surrounded by the modern part of the city and is a great place for people watching. Stockholm is very conscious of the effect of development on the environment and building is carefully controlled, resulting in a city that is clean and green.

Norwegian Blotkake

In Norway any celebration includes Blotkake, especially Syttende Mai (May 17), Norwegian Constitution Day. It's the time of year that the intensely flavored locally grown strawberries are just coming into season.

Serves 10 to 12

Cake

1 cup	cake flour		1 cup	sugar
1 teaspoon	baking powder		1 teaspoon	vanilla
1/4 teaspoon	salt		2 tablespoons	water
4 large	eggs, room temperature			

Frosting/Filling

1 pound	strawberries		1 tablespoon	sugar
2 teaspoons	sugar		1 teaspoon	vanilla
1 1/2 cups	heavy whipping cream			

Heat the oven to 350°F and place the rack in the middle of the oven. Line the bottoms of 2 9-inch baking pans with parchment or waxed paper. Lightly spray liners with nonstick cooking spray.

Sift the cake flour, baking powder and salt into a small bowl.

Place the eggs, 2 teaspoons sugar and vanilla in the bowl of a heavy-duty electric mixer. Beat on medium, with whisk attachment, until foamy. Increase speed to high and beat until thick and lemon colored, about 5 minutes. This mixture will form a thick ribbon that dissolves when the beater is lifted.

Gently fold in half of the flour mixture, the water and the remaining flour. Divide the batter into the prepared pans. Spread evenly.

Bake 20 to 22 minutes or until center springs back when lightly touched. Cool 10 minutes on wire cooling rack. Loosen sides of cake from pans and invert onto rack. Carefully peel off paper. Turn layers right side up and cool completely.

Sort strawberries, saving the prettiest berries for the top of the cake. Slice remaining berries and sprinkle with 1 tablespoon sugar. Let stand about 15 minutes until juicy.

Beat the whipping cream in the bowl of a heavy-duty electric mixer on medium-high with the whisk attachment until soft peaks form.

Place 1 layer of the cake on a serving dish. Top with the sugared strawberries and spread with about 1 cup whipped cream. Add the second layer and spread with the remaining whipped cream. Garnish with the reserved strawberries. Cake must be refrigerated.

Constitution Day in Sandefjord, Norway
Are Karlsen/Shutterstock.com

Norwegian Constitution Day

Norwegian Constitution Day is celebrated on May 17, Syttende Mai. Blotkake, Norwegian Cream Cake slathered with whipped cream and topped with rows of strawberries or raspberries and blueberries, the colors of the Norwegian flag, is an important part of any celebration. This celebration is similar to the American 4th of July. Everyone wears red, white and blue and many march in parades.

This day commemorates the signing of the Norwegian Constitution in 1914, which declared Norway to be an independent nation. All over Norway, elementary school districts arrange a parade with marching bands and children parading through the community. The longest parade is in Oslo, where as many as 100,00 people travel to the city to participate in the festivities.

Chocolate Almond Torte

There are few chocolate desserts in Scandinavian cookbooks, but this creamy torte with chewy almonds is always popular. A torte is usually a dense moist cake with little or no flour. In this recipe ground almonds replace the flour.

SERVES 10

4 ounces	bittersweet chocolate, chopped		4 large	eggs, separated
			3/4 cup	sugar
2 ounces	unsweetened chocolate, chopped		1/2 cup	ground almonds
			3 tablespoons	strong cold coffee
10 tablespoons	unsalted butter		1 teaspoon	vanilla

Heat the oven to 350°F and place the rack in the middle of the oven. Line the bottom of a 9-inch springform pan with parchment paper. Lightly spray the sides of the pan with nonstick cooking spray.

Melt the chocolate and butter in the top of a double boiler until smooth. Cool to room temperature. Lightly beat the egg yolks in a large bowl. Stir in the chocolate, sugar, almonds, coffee and vanilla.

Beat the egg whites in the large bowl of heavy-duty mixer, with whisk attachment, until soft peaks form. (See "Baking with Eggs," page 25.) Stir about 1/4 into the chocolate mixture to lighten it. Fold in the remaining whites. Pour into the springform pan, smoothing the top.

Bake 20 to 25 minutes or until a toothpick inserted about 2 inches from the edge comes out clean. The center will still be moist and jiggle when the pan is gently shaken. Don't worry about cracks, as they will disappear as the cake cools. Cool completely on a wire cooling rack. As it cools the center of this cake will fall. When cool, loosen the sides of the pan and place on serving plate. Cover and chill until serving, at least 4 hours. Top with whipped cream and chocolate curls, if desired.

BAKER'S TIP: Cakes baked in springform pan are often served on the bottom of the pan after removing the sides. Using parchment allows the cake to be removed and placed on a serving plate.

Use slivered or whole almonds and grind in a food processor. Pulse almonds until finely ground. Do not pulse too much or nuts will liquefy.

The Tea Garden at the Old Town Museum in Aarhus
Den Gamle By/Denmark Media Center

AARHUS, DENMARK

Aarhus is the second largest city in Denmark and the principal Danish port. It is located in the geographical center of the country in Jutland, at the mouth of the Aarhus river. Because of its location on the eastern side of the peninsula, it is ideally situated for trade with Sweden, Germany and the Baltic countries.

The oldest archeological ruins date to the end of the 7th century and include half-buried Viking longhouses that were used as homes and workshops. Artifacts such as combs, jewelry and tools date from around the year 900. During the Viking era there was a bridge between the open sea and the protected harbor. When attacked, the bridge would be raised and the ships would be protected, even if the town burned.

The Old Town Museum is an open air museum comprising 75 historical buildings, mostly half-timbered, collected from all parts of Denmark. When opened in 1914, the museum was the first open air museum of its kind. The oldest building dates from 1550 but most of the structures are from the mid 18th to early 19th centuries. The museum was designed to provide a look at Danish urban life in the past, including the Mayor's House, the Merchant Mansion and the house of a nobleman.

Glominge Torte

Almond slices and sweet meringue are the surprising topping on this popular sponge cake. Because the almonds are baked into the meringue, they remain in place when the cakes are inverted to remove the paper liners.

SERVES 10 TO 12

1 cup	all-purpose flour		1/4 cup	milk
1 teaspoon	baking powder		3/4 cup + 1 tbsp	sugar
1/4 teaspoon	salt		1/2 cup	sliced almonds
1/2 cup	unsalted butter, softened		1 cup	heavy whipping cream
1 cup	confectioners' sugar		1/2 teaspoon	pure almond extract
1 teaspoon	pure vanilla			
4 large	eggs, separated			

Heat the oven to 350°F and place the rack in the middle of the oven. Line the bottoms of 2 9-inch baking pans with parchment or waxed paper. Lightly spray paper with nonstick cooking spray.

Combine the flour, baking powder and salt in a small bowl.

Beat the butter until creamy in the bowl of a heavy-duty mixer on medium speed. Gradually add the confectioners' sugar and beat until very light, about 2 minutes. Beat in the vanilla. Beat in egg yolks, 1 at a time, beating well and scraping down sides of the bowl after each. Continue beating on medium for 2 minutes. Add flour mixture in 3 additions alternating with milk in 2 additions. Divide the batter into the prepared pans. Spread evenly. It will be a thin layer of batter.

Beat the egg whites in a clean bowl of heavy-duty mixer, with whisk attachment, on medium speed until soft peaks just begin to form. Gradually beat in 3/4 cup sugar, 1 tablespoon at a time. Beat on high speed until very stiff and glossy, about 3 to 4 minutes, scraping down the sides of the bowl occasionally. Spread the meringue over the cake batter. Sprinkle with the almonds.

Bake 20 to 22 minutes or until the center springs back when lightly touched. The meringue will be lightly browned and no longer moist. Cool 10 minutes on wire cooling rack. Loosen sides of cake from pans and invert onto rack. Carefully peel off paper. Turn layers right side up and cool completely.

Beat the whipping cream in the bowl of a heavy-duty electric mixer with the whisk attachment on medium-high speed until soft peaks form. Beat in remaining 1 tablespoon sugar and the almond extract.

Place 1 layer of the cake on a serving dish. Spread with whipped cream. Cover with second layer. Chill until serving.

Windmill in South Sweden
Kai Schirmer/Shutterstock.com

BAKING WITH EGGS

Eggs are a crucial part of successful baking, providing structure, richness and leavening. Recipes are developed using large eggs unless otherwise specified.

It is easier to separate the whites and yolks when eggs are cold. After separating, cover the yolks and refrigerate and allow the whites to come to room temperature. When using whole eggs, allow the eggs to stand at room temperature about 30 minutes before beating or place cold eggs in a bowl of very warm water for about 15 minutes.

For egg whites to whip the highest, be sure there is no yolk present and that the bowl is free of any grease. Beat egg whites on medium-high using the whisk attachment, if you have one, until they are foamy and just beginning to form soft peaks. Soft peaks hold their shape well but droop a little when the beaters are lifted. Gradually, begin adding sugar at this point and continue beating on high speed until the sugar dissolves and stiff glossy peaks are formed that remain when the beaters are lifted.

Overbeaten egg whites become curdy and lumpy and liquid separates out and they are hard to fold in without losing air.

Sans Rival Torte

This elaborate dessert relies on several important techniques: making hard meringue, caramelizing nuts and creating a classic French or Italian buttercream. Doing it one step at a time is the key to success.

SERVES 8 TO 10

1 1/4 cups	superfine sugar	1/2 teaspoon	vanilla
1 tablespoon	cornstarch	1/2 teaspoon	almond extract
4 large	egg whites, room temperature	1/2 cup	sugar
1/2 teaspoon	cream of tartar	1/2 cup	sliced almonds

Buttercream

1 1/2 cups	unsalted butter, softened	1 cup	sugar
4 large	egg yolks	1/2 cup	water
		1 teaspoon	vanilla

Drottningholm Palace, Stockholm, Sweden
Mordechai Meiri/Shutterstock.com

DROTTNINGHOLM PALACE, SWEDEN

Drottningholm Palace is the current private residence of the royal family of Sweden. It was built in the 1660s by Queen Dowager Hedwig as a summer residence. After its completion, it hosted the court for many years in the seventeenth and eighteenth century and is often called "Sweden's Versailles." Taking a ferry from Stockholm is the perfect way to visit.

Heat the oven to 300°F. Line 2 baking sheets with parchment paper and draw three 7 1/2-inch squares. Place drawing side down on baking sheets. Stagger the oven racks in the oven. (The squares can be 7 to 8 inches. It's important to bake all 3 layers at 1 time, so 2 squares must fit on 1 baking sheet.)

Make the meringue. Whisk the superfine sugar and the cornstarch together in a small bowl. Using the whisk attachment, beat the egg whites in a large bowl until foamy and beat in the cream of tartar, vanilla and almond extract. Beat until soft peaks form. Gradually add the sugar mixture, 1 tablespoon at a time, beating on high speed until the sugar mixture is dissolved and the meringue holds stiff glossy peaks when the beater is lifted, 4 to 6 minutes.

Spoon the meringue in 3 mounds onto the parchment and spread evenly to the drawn edges using a metal spatula. Place in the oven and reduce the heat to 250°F. Bake for 22 to 27 minutes or until firm and dry to the touch. Any cracks may look slightly moist. Remove and cool completely on a wire cooling rack. When cool, carefully peel off the paper. (I find it easier to remove the paper if I trim it 1/2 inch larger than the meringue.)

Melt the 1/2 cup sugar in a small nonstick skillet over low heat. Add the almonds and continue cooking until the sugar is golden brown and coats the almonds. Pour hot almonds onto a well-buttered baking sheet. Cool completely and crush into small pieces. (You can use a small processor.)

To make the buttercream, cream the butter well in a small bowl. The butter should be at a cool room temperature. Beat the egg yolks in the bowl of a heavy-duty mixer using the whisk attachment until lightened and creamy about 1 minute.

Combine 1 cup sugar and 1/2 cup water in a small saucepan. Cook over medium high heat until temperature reaches 230°F. (For best results use a candy thermometer.) Very slowly, drizzle syrup in a steady stream into the egg yolks beating constantly on high. Try not to get any syrup on the sides of the bowl. Scrape down the sides of the bowl and continue beating until the bowl

is cool, 3 to 4 minutes. Add the butter mixture slowly, about 1 tablespoon at a time, beating in each piece before adding another. Beat until smooth and light. Add 1/2 cup of crushed praline.

Place 1 layer of the meringue on a serving dish. Spread with 1/3 of the buttercream. Repeat 2 times. Decorate top with the remaining praline.

Store torte in the refrigerator but allow to stand at room temperature about 1/2 hour before serving to soften the buttercream.

BAKER'S TIP: To use granulated sugar in place of superfine sugar, place 1 1/4 cups + 1 1/2 teaspoons granulated sugar in a food processor. Process several seconds until the sugar is finely ground.

You may test the temperature of the sugar/water syrup using the soft ball test. Drop a small amount of syrup into a cup of cold water. When it forms a soft ball that holds its shape it is between 234°F and 242°F.

If the buttercream separates, beat 1 or 2 tablespoons softened butter into it on high speed and beat until creamy.

Strawberry Cream Cakeroll

As the centerpiece of a dessert table or the finale to a festive summertime meal, this cake is guaranteed to impress your guests. Be sure to roll the cake when it is just out of the oven and warm. You can reduce the whipping cream in the filling to 1 1/2 cups, but I prefer lots of strawberries and cream.

Christmas in Tivoli
Kim Wyon/VisitDenmark.com

Serves 8 to 10

3/4 cup	cake flour
3/4 cup + 1 tbsp	sugar
4	large eggs, room temperature
1/4 teaspoon	salt
1/4 teaspoon	cream of tartar
1 tablespoon	water
1 teaspoon	vanilla
3 cups	chopped strawberries (1/2-inch pieces)
1 tablespoon	sugar
1 (8 oz) package	cream cheese, softened
1 1/2 cups	confectioners' sugar, sifted
1 teaspoon	vanilla
2 cups	heavy whipping cream

Heat oven to 350°F and place the rack in the middle of the oven. Line a 15 x 10 x 1-inch jellyroll pan with parchment paper. Spray parchment with nonstick cooking spray including sides of pan.

Sift the cake flour with 1 tablespoon sugar.

Place eggs, 3/4 cup sugar, salt, cream of tartar, water and vanilla in a large bowl. Beat on medium, with whisk attachment, until foamy. Increase speed to high and beat until thick and lemon colored, about 5 minutes. This mixture will form a thick ribbon that dissolves when the beater is lifted.

Fold in the cake flour and mix until flour disappears. Pour into the prepared pan and spread evenly. Bake 16 to 18 minutes or until center springs back when touched lightly with a finger and cake is lightly browned.

While the cake is baking, place a clean linen towel on a work surface and sift confectioners' sugar generously over entire surface.

Immediately after removing the cake from the oven, loosen the sides of the cake and invert it onto the towel. Carefully peel off the parchment paper and roll up using the towel. Starting at the short end, roll the cake and towel together. Place on wire cooling rack and cool to room temperature, about 1 hour.

Mix the strawberries with the sugar in a medium bowl and let stand 15 minutes. Beat the cream cheese on medium in a large bowl until smooth. Gradually beat in the 1 1/2 cup confectioners' sugar and vanilla. Scrape down the sides of the bowl. Gradually beat in the whipping cream on low. Beat on high using whisk attachment until soft peaks form. Beat in strawberries for 1 minute, breaking up the strawberries.

Unroll the cake. Spread about 1 1/2 cups strawberry cream over cake, spreading to edges. Gently roll up. Place seam side down on serving plate. Cover the top and sides with the remaining

Denmark's Tivoli Garden

Tivoli Gardens is the world's second oldest amusement park and the most visited site in Denmark. When it opened in 1843 it only had two rides—a roller coaster and a horse drawn carousel. When Georg Carstensen asked King Christian VIII for permission to open the park it was to be a place for music, performances, entertainment, alehouses and restaurants. After dark it is famous for illuminations and fireworks. Tivoli Lake is a remnant of the old city moat, but as the city grew the park became central as opposed to outside the city gates. Today it is lit by 115,000 bulbs and 25 different styles of lamps.

In 1944 several of the buildings were burnt to the ground supposedly by the Nazis who were occupying Denmark at the time in retaliation for the bombing of a Danish company that was producing weapons for the Germans. It was an attempt to break the Danish spirit but the buildings were quickly rebuilt, as they are an important part of the national pride.

Tivoli Gardens is constantly changing in order to make room for new rides and restaurants but remains true its roots as a place for entertainment and amusement.

strawberry cream. Chill at least 2 hours before serving. Cut cake into slices using a serrated knife. Store in the refrigerator.

Frystekake

Known as Norwegian Royal Cake, this pastry seems very plain, but the tender, buttery crust and chewy almond filling are addictive. First sold in the 1860s at Erichsen's Konditori in Trondheim, it has become a Norwegian favorite. Serve it in thin slices with coffee or tea for an afternoon break or for a sweet ending to a meal.

SERVES 8 TO 10

1 3/4 cups	all-purpose flour	1 1/2 cups	sliced almonds
1/3 cup	sugar	1 1/4 cups	confectioners' sugar
1 teaspoon	baking powder		
1/4 teaspoon	salt	2 tablespoons	heavy whipping cream
1/2 cup	unsalted butter, cut up	2 teaspoons	dark rum or vanilla extract
2 large	eggs, separated		
4 teaspoons	milk		

Heat the oven to 350°F. Place the oven rack in the center of the oven.

Make the crust. Place the flour, sugar, baking powder and salt in a food processor bowl and pulse briefly to mix. Add the butter and process until coarse crumbs form with some pea-sized pieces. Scrape down the sides of the bowl. Combine 1 egg yolk and the milk. With the processor running, add the yolk and milk and process until dough begins to clump together, 15 to 30 seconds. If dough doesn't form, add milk 1 teaspoon at a time until dough forms.

Put the dough on well-floured work surface and gather it together into a ball. Wrap in waxed paper and chill about an hour.

Place the almonds in the food processor bowl and pulse until finely ground. When the almonds are finely ground add the confectioners' sugar, whipping cream, 2 egg whites and rum. Pulse briefly to mix.

Reserve about 1/2 dough and place in refrigerator. Press the remaining dough into the bottom and up the sides of a 9-inch tart pan with removable bottom. If the dough is sticky, dip your fingers into a little flour. Spread the almond filling into the crust.

On a well-floured surface, roll the remaining dough to 1/8 inch thickness. Cut into strips about 3/4 inch wide. Place strips in a lattice on top of the filling, pressing onto sides. Mix remaining egg yolk with 1 teaspoon water and brush onto strips of pastry.

Bake 28 to 32 minutes or until light golden brown. Cool on wire cooling rack. Remove sides of pan before serving.

BAKER'S TIP: This very tender dough breaks easily when it is rolled. Just place the strips over the filling and they will bake together.

Bergen Waterfront
Jens Henrik Nybo/VisitNorway.com

BERGEN, NORWAY

Bergen in western Norway is considered the gateway to the fjords and is situated between the Sognefjord and the Hardangerfjord. The area is filled with breathtaking views of snow-covered mountains sparkling with large and small waterfalls. Norway has the largest number of fjords in the world and they are listed on UNESCO's World Heritage List.

As glaciers retreated, the deep valleys filled with salt water, creating scenic beauty and playgrounds for seals and porpoises. Sognefjord is the deepest, dropping 1308 meters below sea level, and Bergen is the perfect place from which to explore its beauty. From Bergen there are ferries to other inland fishing villages and medieval stave churches. In the center of town there is a flight of steps leading to the water. These were build for Kaiser Wilhelm, who vacationed here from 1899 to the start of WWI. Because of the Gulf Stream, the fjords enjoy a mild climate and remain almost ice free.

Finnland
Johan Wildhagen/VisitNorway.com

PUDDINGS & CUSTARDS

Rich, eggy and silky smooth or slightly tart and bursting with fruit flavor, puddings are cozy home-style desserts and to me, the ultimate comfort food. Many of these simple sweets are made with foods that you probably have on hand: milk, eggs and sugar. Flan, or baked custard, and puddings have the creamiest texture when prepared with whole milk. Using skim milk decreases the fat but also reduces silkiness. Heavy whipping cream adds richness and a level of decadence.

Custards are thickened when the proteins in eggs coagulate, trapping liquid within a net of protein strands. Gentle heat produces creamy results. Overcooking causes the eggs to scramble and "weep" forcing out liquid and creating lumps or curds. To prevent overcooking, use a water bath or *bain marie* when baking custards on low heat.

To bake custard in a water bath, find a container that is about 2 inches larger than the baking dish or custard cups. Place the pan for the water bath (a roasting pan is a good choice) on the oven rack. Add the baking dish or custard cups and add hot water to the large pan surrounding the baking dish. Carefully, slide the rack into the oven, without spilling water into the custard or pudding. It's also important to keep potholders out of the water because once wet they conduct heat well and are no longer effective.

To test for doneness, insert a knife about 2/3 of the way from the side to the center. The knife will come out wet but clean. The center of the custard should still jiggle slightly. Remove the baked custards from the water bath as soon as they are cool enough to handle in order to prevent overcooking.

Whether stirred or baked, these puddings will become family favorites and are easy to prepare for company or weeknight meals.

Caramel Flan

A richly flavored caramel sauce bakes in the bottom of the dish underneath the creamy custard, also known as Brule Pudding. When the pudding is released from the dish, it bathes the dessert in a delicate sauce. One of my Swedish friends says this is a favorite from his childhood, one his dad always requested for his birthday.

SERVES 9

1 1/4 cups	sugar, divided		1/8 teaspoon	salt
3 tablespoons	water		1 teaspoon	vanilla
2 drops	lemon juice		2 1/2 cups	whole milk
4	large eggs, beaten			

Heat the oven to 350°F. Place the oven rack in the center of the oven. Butter the bottom of a 9-inch pie plate.

Cook 3/4 cup sugar, the water and lemon juice in a small saucepan over medium-high heat until most of the sugar is dissolved. Swirl the liquid around the sides of the pan to dissolve any remaining sugar crystals. Reduce the heat to medium and cook until the syrup turns a deep golden color, 3 to 4 minutes. Immediately remove from the heat and pour into the pie plate.

Combine the eggs, remaining 1/2 cup sugar, salt and vanilla and mix until smooth. Stir in the milk. Pour through a strainer into the pie plate.

Place the pie plate in a large roasting pan. Add hot water to a depth of about 1/2 inch. Bake 35 to 40 minutes or until almost set in the center. It will still wobble a little in the middle.

Carefully remove the custard from the water and cool on a wire cooling rack. Run a knife around the edges to prevent custard from cracking. Refrigerate until chilled, at least 4 hours or overnight.

Carefully loosen the edges and invert onto a serving plate. Cut into wedges and spoon caramel over each serving.

BAKER'S TIP: It's important to cook the sugar syrup until the color changes to a deep caramel. Cook slowly or the syrup will turn dark and will taste like burnt sugar.

Stockholm City Hall,
Site of the Nobel Prize Winners' Dinner and Dance
vetpathologist/Shutterstock.com

NOBEL PRIZE

The Nobel Prize, the world's most prestigious award, was established by Alfred Nobel in his last will and testament written in 1895. After reading his supposed obituary in a French newspaper (his brother Ludvig had died) under the headline "The Merchant of Death is Dead," he was concerned of how he would be remembered in history. Nobel's most famous invention was dynamite which enabled many countries to build canals, railways and tunnels at the turn of the 20th century, a time of great development as well as war.

As an engineer and inventor, he had amassed a large fortune and decided to use it to award prizes to those whose achievements had the "greatest benefit on mankind." His fortune is managed by the Nobel Foundation and the cash value of the Nobel Prize in 2012 was over $1 million. The awards are given in the fields of physics, chemistry, medicine, literature and peace and were first awarded in 1901. In 1968 an award in Economics was added. All of the prizes are awarded by the Royal Swedish Academy of Sciences, the Karolinska Institute, or the Swedish Academy except for the Nobel Peace Prize. The Nobel Peace Prize is awarded by the Norwegian Nobel Committee and presented in Oslo.

Aunt Else's Rice Pudding

Don't forget the almond! It's brings good luck. There are several traditions involving the finder of the almond in the rice pudding. Sometimes a marzipan pig is awarded to the winner who can also expect good luck for the next year. Another tradition is that whoever finds the almond in their serving will be married within the year. If a child finds the almond, they are usually given a treat. Serve pudding in a large bowl and let everyone serve himself or herself looking for the hidden almond!

SERVES 6 TO 8

4 cups	whole milk
1/2 cup	long grain rice
1/2 cup	sugar
2 large	eggs, well beaten
1/2 cup	heavy whipping cream
1	whole almond

Heat the milk in the top of a double boiler until small bubbles form on the sides of the pan. Add the rice and cook, stirring occasionally, until the rice is tender. This will take 1 1/2 to 2 hours. Once the sugar is added, the rice will not soften further. Stir in the sugar and continue cooking about 30 minutes or until the pudding thickens slightly.

Combine the eggs and cream in a small bowl and beat with a whisk until smooth. Very slowly add to the rice while stirring rapidly. Continue cooking, stirring constantly, until the pudding thickens. Remove from the heat and stir in the vanilla. Add the almond.

Cool to room temperature and chill. Serve with fruit or sprinkle with cinnamon before serving.

BAKER'S TIP: You can make a double boiler, also called a *bain marie*, by placing a small saucepan inside a medium saucepan that has about an inch of water. Check occasionally and add water as needed. By using a double boiler, the pudding doesn't need to be stirred constantly.

Lingonberries, the Forest Cranberry
mrivserg/Shutterstock.com

LINGONBERRIES

Lingonberries, also called cowberries in some areas, grow abundantly in Scandinavia and other northern European countries with cooler climates. They do not grow well in warm summers. They grow wild on a tree-like shrub and can be easily harvested throughout the northern forests by anyone willing to pick and clean the berries.

Because they are high in Vitamin C, beta-carotene and many minerals and phytochemicals, they are an important nutritional supplement to the diet. Highly acidic, older generations were able to preserve them simply by placing them in water. Lingonberries are similar to cranberries but are juicier and tarter, so most often they are sweetened before serving. Sometimes only sugar is added but they can also be made into preserves or jam. Traditionally, they are served with meats and meatballs or cooked into compotes, syrups or liqueurs.

Norwegian Rommegrot

SERVES 6

1/2 cup	unsalted butter	1/2 teaspoon	salt
1/2 cup	all-purpose flour	4 cups	whole milk
1/2 cup	sugar		

Cook the butter in a medium saucepan over medium-low heat until melted. Stir in the flour until it is absorbed. Cook 1 minute, stirring constantly. Add the sugar, salt and milk and continue cooking, stirring constantly, until the mixture comes to a complete boil. Reduce heat to low and simmer 1 minute, stirring constantly.

Remove the pan from the heat and cool slightly or chill until serving. Sprinkle lightly with cinnamon, sugar, brown sugar or melted butter. You can also top it with raisins.

BAKER'S TIP: I have the best results when I add the milk all at once while mixing with a wire whisk. If the flour isn't evenly mixed into the milk, the pudding will be lumpy. Press a piece of plastic wrap or waxed paper to the surface to prevent a skin from forming on the top as it cools.

Cinnamon Apple Bread Pudding

SERVES 8

1/3 cup	unsalted butter	1/2 cup	sugar
1/2 cup	brown sugar, firmly-packed	1 teaspoon	vanilla
2	apples, peeled, cored and sliced (about 2 cups)	3 large	eggs
		2 cups	2% milk
1 teaspoon	cinnamon	6 cups	1-inch pieces of day-old French bread (about 8 ounces)

Butter a 2-quart or 11 x 7-inch baking dish or spray with nonstick cooking spray.

Melt butter in large nonstick skillet over medium heat and stir in brown sugar. Add apples and sprinkle with cinnamon. Cook until the apples begin to soften, about 3 minutes. Spread into the bottom of the prepared dish.

Beat sugar, vanilla, and eggs in a large bowl until blended. Slowly beat in milk. Strain through a mesh strainer, if desired. Add the bread cubes and mix. Spoon over the apples. Let stand at room temperature about 15 to 30 minutes or until the bread has absorbed the milk mixture. Press any bread that is not moistened into the liquid.

Heat the oven to 350°F. Place the rack in the middle of the oven. Bake 45 to 55 minutes or until set in the center and a knife inserted near the center comes out clean, although it will be wet.

Cool slightly before serving warm or cool to room temperature and refrigerate. To serve, cut pudding into squares and place in individual serving dishes.

Cherry Pancake Pudding

SERVES 6 TO 8

2 cups	pitted dark sweet cherries (16-ounce can), drained and patted dry		1/3 cup	sugar
			1/4 teaspoon	salt
			3	eggs
			1 teaspoon	vanilla
1 tablespoon	sugar		2/3 cup	all-purpose flour
1 tablespoon	dark rum, optional			Confectioners' sugar
1 cup	2% milk			

Heat the oven to 375°F. Place the oven rack in the center of the oven. Butter the bottom of a 9-inch pie plate.

Place the cherries in the pie plate and sprinkle with 1 tablespoon sugar and the rum.

Combine the milk, 1/3 cup sugar, salt, eggs, vanilla and flour in a blender container. Blend 10 seconds. Scrape down the sides of the container and blend until smooth. Pour over the cherries.

Bake 10 minutes and reduce the oven to 350°F. Continue baking 25 to 30 minutes or until the pancake is golden brown and set in center. A knife inserted in the center will come out clean, although it will be wet. Sprinkle with confectioners' sugar and cut into wedges. Serve warm. Refrigerate any leftovers.

Danish Red Fruit Pudding

SERVES 4 TO 6

3 cups	chopped rhubarb		1/4 cup	cornstarch
2 cups	sliced strawberries		1 cup	heavy whipping cream
3 1/3 cups	water, divided			
1 cup	sugar			
1 teaspoon	freshly squeezed lemon juice			

Combine the rhubarb, strawberries, 3 cups water, sugar and lemon juice in a medium saucepan. Cook over medium heat until the mixture comes to a boil. Reduce the heat to low and simmer 10 to 15 minutes or until fruit is very tender. Press through a fine-mesh sieve, saving the juice. Discard the solids. Rinse out the saucepan and return the juice to the pan.

Combine the cornstarch and remaining 1/3 cup water in a small bowl and stir until the cornstarch is dissolved. Stir into the fruit juice, stirring constantly. Cook over medium heat, stirring constantly until the mixture comes to a boil and thickens. Boil 1 minute, stirring constantly. Divide into serving bowls and chill at least 2 hours.

Beat the whipping cream in the bowl of a heavy-duty electric mixer with the whisk attachment until soft peaks form. Top each serving with cream. You can also pour heavy cream over the chilled pudding.

BAKER'S TIP: Pressing plastic wrap or waxed paper to the surface of the pudding will prevent a skin from forming.

Baked Rice Pudding

Because rice had to be imported in the 1800s, it was expensive. For this reason, it was only served on special occasions and celebrations. Unlike some rice puddings that need to be stirred while cooking, you can relax while it bakes. Keeping with tradition, add a whole almond and reward the lucky winner who finds it in their serving.

SERVES 6 TO 8

1 1/2 cups	water		1/2 cup	sugar
3/4 cup	Arborio or short grain rice		3	large eggs, well beaten
1/4 teaspoon	coarse salt		1 teaspoon	pure vanilla
4 cups	hot whole milk		1/2 cup	raisins

Bring the water to a boil in a medium saucepan and add the rice and salt. Cover and reduce heat to low. Simmer 15 to 20 minutes or until the water is absorbed.

Heat the oven to 350°F. Place the rack in the center of the oven. Butter a 2-quart baking dish.

Combine the milk, sugar, eggs and vanilla in a large bowl and beat until well blended. Stir in the rice and raisins, mixing quickly to prevent the eggs from cooking. Pour into the baking dish. Set the baking dish in a larger pan and add boiling water to the outer pan to a depth of about 1/2 inch. (See page 33 for directions on making a water bath.)

Bake 55 to 65 minutes or until knife inserted in the center comes out clean, although it will be wet. Stir after about 30 minutes, if desired. Serve warm or cool to room temperature and refrigerate.

Aurora Borealis, The Northern Lights
Jorg Hackemann/Shutterstock.com

AURORA BOREALIS

Because of its geographic location in northern Europe, the aurora borealis is often visible in Scandinavia. In Finland, this Technicolor spectacle can be taken for granted because it occurs as many as 200 nights of the year, if the weather is clear.

This natural phenomenon is created by electrons blown toward earth by solar winds interacting with the earth's atmosphere. They are overhead the magnetic North Pole, which in lower latitudes causes them to appear as a green or red glow in the northern sky.

The name aurora borealis refers to the Roman goddess of dawn, Aurora, and Boreas, the Greek name for the north wind. Also called the Northern Lights, the predominant color is green but they also appear in reds; they can vary in intensity; and sometimes they appear briefly and other times, they glow for hours. The best time of year to view this theater in the sky is late autumn, winter and early spring, between the autumn and spring equinox. The United States (mostly Alaska), Canada and Scotland are the other countries in northern latitudes where this brilliant display is sometimes visible.

Relaxing on a Moonlit Evening, Denmark
Neils Thye/VisitDenmark.com

POACHED PEAR
WITH CARDAMOM CREAM

PEACH ALMOND CRUMBLE

BLUEBERRY RHUBARB TRIFLE

SCANDINAVIAN WINTER FRUIT SOUP

FINNISH BLUEBERRY TART

RHUBARB CUSTARD TART

COUNTRY STYLE PEAR TART

MAZARIN TARTS

LEMON MOUSSE

HAZELNUT MERINGUE
WITH RASPBERRIES

DANISH AEBLEKAGE

TARTS & FRUIT DESSERTS

DENMARK, NORWAY, SWEDEN, FINLAND AND ICELAND HAVE SIMILAR GROWING SEASONS and similar crops because they share the same geographical features. Short summers with long days result in berries and fruits with intense flavors. The produce of the land, including cream and butter from dairy farms, is the basis for most Scandinavian desserts. Almonds are present in almost everything—sliced, slivered or ground. Almond paste is often used as a filling, adding a chewy texture and a bittersweet flavor.

Early in the season, rhubarb's tart, tangy flavor appears in many desserts, especially in compotes or sauces. Hazelnut Meringue is topped with fresh local raspberries and enriched with whipped cream, The Finns pick wild blueberries in the forests and use them to fill tarts with cookie-like crusts such as the Finnish Blueberry Tart. Whipped cream is the finishing touch at the end of many meals and may be delicately flavored as it is for Poached Pear with Cardamom Cream. Norwegian Fruit Soup is prepared in the winter when fresh fruit is scarce and dried fruits are available.

Always use fresh fruit, local when possible, and ideally, without blemishes. Because berries are fragile and spoil quickly, store them in the refrigerator and use them as soon as possible. Peaches and pears often require a couple of days at room temperature to complete ripening. Place them in a paper bag and check for ripeness every day. Ripe peaches will be fragrant and yield to soft pressure. Because pears ripen from the inside out, press gently on the stem end to judge ripeness.

Scandinavian desserts focus on seasonally available fruits enriched with dairy products such as butter and cream. They provide the perfect endings to meals without adding an overwhelming sweetness.

Poached Pears
with Cardamom Cream

D'Anjou pears or Bosc pears are the two varieties I find the best for baking. D'Anjou are not available year round but I can usually find Bosc. Pears should be firm and just beginning to soften at the stem end.

SERVES 4

4	firm medium D'Anjou or Bosc pears	1/2 cup	heavy whipping cream
8	cups water	2 teaspoons	sugar
2	cups sugar	1/4 teaspoon	ground cardamom
1	orange		Caramel sauce

Place the water and 2 cups sugar in a 3 to 4 quart saucepan and cook over medium heat, stirring to dissolve the sugar. Remove the peel from the orange with a vegetable peeler, avoiding the white pith. Add to the pan. Squeeze the juice from the orange and add to the pan.

Using a melon baller or an apple corer, remove the core and seeds from the pears. Work from the bottom of the pears and leave the stems intact. Add to the saucepan and bring the liquid to a boil. Cover and reduce heat to low. Gently simmer pears 5 to 10 minutes or until they begin to soften. Remove pan from the heat and let the pears cool in the syrup.

Beat the whipping cream in the bowl of a heavy-duty electric mixer with the whisk attachment until soft peaks form. Add the sugar and cardamom and continue beating until the sugar is dissolved.

Serve pears with whipped cream and caramel sauce.

The National Gallery in Oslo
Dag Ivarsøy/Innovation Norway

THE NATIONAL GALLERY

The National Gallery was established in 1842 following a parliamentary decision in 1836. Originally located in the Royal Palace, Oslo, it got its own museum building in 1882, designed by Heinrich Ernst and Adolf Schirmer.

The National Gallery houses Norway's largest public collection of paintings, drawings and sculptures. The museum's central attractions include Edvard Munch's The Scream *and* Madonna *and paintings by Cézanne and Manet.*

The museum's exhibitions present older art, with principal emphasis on art from Norway. The permanent exhibition shows highlights from the collection and national icons from the romantic period until the mid-1900s.

Peach Almond Crumble

Peaches are my favorite summer fruit. When buying fresh peaches, I have found the best way to judge quality is by smelling the fruit. Peaches that aren't fragrant usually won't ripen properly. If it doesn't smell like a peach, it probably won't taste like a peach. I always place fresh peaches in a paper bag to ripen a couple of days before I use them.

Reykjavík Skyline
VisitIceland.com

SERVES 6 TO 8

6 cups	sliced, peeled peaches (about 6 medium)		1/4 cup	sugar
			1/8 teaspoon	salt
1 tablespoon	lemon juice		1/4 cup	cold unsalted butter
2 tablespoons	sugar			
1 tablespoon	cornstarch		1/3 cup	old-fashioned rolled oats
1 teaspoon	almond extract			
1/3 cup	all-purpose flour		1/3 cup	sliced almonds

Heat the oven to 375°F. Place the oven rack in the center of the oven. Lightly butter a 1 1/2 quart baking dish (or a 9 x 9-inch baking dish).

Peel and slice the peaches into a large bowl and toss with lemon juice to prevent browning.

Combine the sugar and cornstarch in a small bowl and stir into the peaches. Add the almond extract and toss gently to mix. Spoon the peaches into the lightly buttered baking dish.

To make the crumb topping, combine the flour, sugar and salt in a medium bowl. Cut in the butter with a pastry blender until the mixture resembles coarse crumbs. Stir in the oatmeal and almonds. Sprinkle over the peaches.

Bake 50 to 60 minutes or until the topping is browned and the juices have thickened. If you are using a deep dish or casserole, you may need to bake a little longer. The juices should be thick and bubbling in the center.

Serve warm or at room temperature with ice cream or whipping cream.

BAKER'S TIP: Peaches peel easily when dipped in boiling water. Bring a large saucepan of water to a boil and add peaches. Let stand 20 seconds and remove. Cool immediately by placing in a bowl of cold water. Peach skins will slip right off.

ICELAND

Iceland is considered one of the Nordic countries because of its location and its many similarities to the countries of Scandinavia. It is the second largest island in Europe, second only to Great Britain. The island was formed by volcanic activity over millions of years, which continues today. Glaciers cover 11% of the land. Volcanic geothermal energy is used to heat homes throughout Iceland.

Iceland was governed by Denmark for many centuries and in 1944, declared its independence. Reykjavik is the northernmost national capital in the world and contains approximately half of the population of the country. The remaining population centers are along the coasts as there are portions of the country that are uninhabitable. Of the total population of about 319,000, many are employed in the tourism or fishing industries.

Iceland had one of the highest standards of living and per capital income until the global financial crisis of 2008, which had a great impact on the economy. Iceland is a parliamentary constitutional republic governed by the Althingi, which is composed of members elected every four years.

Blueberry Rhubarb Trifle

Try different berries or combinations of berries with the tart, tangy rhubarb. For the cake part of the trifle, I recommend the rich buttery Scandinavian Almond Cake. (See page 19.)

SERVES 8

1 cup	water
3/4 cup	sugar
4 cups	chopped fresh or frozen rhubarb
1 cup	fresh blueberries or strawberries
1 1/2 cups	heavy whipping cream
2 tablespoons	sugar

1 teaspoon	pure vanilla
4 cups	cubed cake (almond cake, angel food cake or pound cake)
24	whole blueberries or 8 strawberries

Place the water and sugar in a medium saucepan and bring to a boil over medium-high heat. Cook 1 minute or until sugar is completely dissolved. Add rhubarb and remove from the heat. Cool 15 minutes and add the blueberries or strawberries. Cool completely.

Beat the whipping cream in the bowl of a heavy-duty electric mixer with the whisk attachment until soft peaks form. Add the sugar and vanilla and continue beating until the sugar is dissolved.

Place 1/4 cup cake cubes in 8 individual serving dishes. Add 1/4 cup rhubarb and a scant 1/4 cup whipped cream. Repeat layers. Garnish each dish with 3 blueberries or strawberries and chill several hours or until serving.

Helsinki Waterfront
VisitFinland.com

THE SAMIS OF LAPLAND

The Samis are the ethnic inhabitants of Lapland and have a unique culture centered on the land. The Lapland region is spread across the northern areas of Sweden, Norway, Finland and Russia. In 1909 Russia annexed a part of eastern Sweden, creating the Grand Duchy of Finland, a division still in effect. Arriving in the area around 1000 years ago, the Samis traded with the Vikings and the Hanseatic League. Samis continue to live a traditional lifestyle centered on reindeer herding. They use reindeer for meat, skins and transportation. The Sami language has 400 words for reindeer showing the importance of this animal to their lives. They also fish along the coastal areas. In addition to herding, an industry has developed making traditional clothing to sell to tourists.

In 1956 the Nordic Sami Council was created to protect, preserve and promote the Sami culture, bringing official recognition to the unique ethnic group. Parts of Lapland, containing some of the most spectacular national parks of Europe, have been named a UNESCO world heritage site. Tourism is increasing in the area since the Ice Hotel opened in Jukikasjarvi. The hotel containing 60 rooms, is open from October to April and is made entirely from ice and snow. Thermal sleeping bags and reindeer skins are provided to guests. Guests are greeted in the morning with a cup of hot lingonberry juice.

Scandinavian Winter Fruit Soup

Serving soup made with dried fruits is a Christmas tradition in many Nordic homes, especially in Norway and Sweden. This recipe makes a large quantity and is perfect for extended family gatherings. You can use any cooking apple but the tartness of Granny Smith apples contrasts nicely with the sweetness of the other fruit.

SERVES 12 TO 16

6 cups	water	6	whole cloves
1/3 cup	instant tapioca	1	orange, cut in half
1 cup	sugar	3	cinnamon sticks
2 cups	chopped peeled cored apples (2 medium)	3 to 4 cups	grape juice or apple cider
2 cups	dried pitted prunes	1 can (16 oz)	pitted dark sweet cherries, drained
1 cup	dried apricots	2 tablespoons	lemon juice
1 cup	golden raisins		

Combine the tapioca and water in a 4-quart Dutch oven or large saucepan. Let stand 15 minutes. Add the sugar, apples, prunes, apricots and raisins. Press the cloves into the orange and add to the pan along with the cinnamon sticks. Bring to a boil over medium-high heat. Reduce the heat to low and cook 20 to 30 minutes or until clear and thick and apples are tender. Remove orange halves and cinnamon sticks.

Stir in grape juice, cherries and lemon juice. Continue cooking until heated through. Cool to room temperature or chill until serving. Serve soup at room temperature or chilled.

Borgund Stave Church
Imfoto/Shutterstock.com

NORWAY'S STAVE CHURCHES

Norway contains the greatest number of stave churches in northern Europe. Dating from the 12th century when other European countries were building lofty stone cathedrals, these places of worship combine Christian designs with Viking motifs such as dragon heads and runes. Their framework is based on the lines of Viking longships, using ancient woodworking techniques.

Around the year 1300, Norway had between 1000 and 2000 stave churches but by the 19th century they had fallen into disrepair. Supported by vertical staves similar to the ribs of a ship, their interior spaces soar to the sky. Buildings using this method of construction could withstand the fierce northern winds by swaying and bending.

The Urnes Stave Church near the Songefjord is the oldest stave church in Norway today and is listed as a prestigious UNESCO World Heritage Site. Formerly the private church of a wealthy family, it is decorated with animal shapes such as elk and doves from the Middle Ages and also ancient designs of centaurs and dragons.

Finnish Blueberry Tart

Wild blueberries are abundant in the forests of Finland and the Finns make good use of these berries in the summer. The slightly sweet cookie-like crust of this tart is filled with a blueberry topping that captures the summertime freshness of just-picked berries. Instead of mounding it with rich cream, you can also serve it with vanilla or cinnamon ice cream.

SERVES 8

CRUST

1 1/4 cups	all-purpose flour		1/2 cup	cold unsalted butter, cut into 1/2 inch pieces
1/4 cup	sugar			
1/4 teaspoon	salt		1	large egg yolk

FILLING

2 pints (4 cups)	blueberries, divided		3 tablespoons	cornstarch
			3 tablespoons	water
1/2 cup	sugar		1 tablespoon	lemon juice

TOPPING

1 cup	heavy whipping cream		1 tablespoon	sugar
			1 teaspoon	vanilla

Heat the oven to 375°F. Place the rack in the lower third of the oven. Lightly grease with shortening and dust with flour a 9-inch tart pan with a removeable bottom.

CRUST

Combine the flour, sugar and salt for the crust in a food processor bowl. Add the cold butter and pulse until the dough resembles coarse crumbs. With the processor running, add the egg yolk. Process until dough starts to clump together, about 15 seconds.

Place the dough on a lightly floured surface and gather into a ball. Place the dough in the center of the prepared tart pan. Using your fingers, press the dough out to the edges of the pan and all the way up the sides. Lightly dust your fingers with a little flour if the dough is sticky.

Pierce the crust generously with a fork. Bake 12 to 15 minutes or until golden brown. Cool on a wire cooling rack.

FILLING

Place 1 cup blueberries in the pastry shell. Combine the sugar and cornstarch in a medium saucepan. Add the remaining 3 cups blueberries, water and lemon juice and mix. Bring to a boil over medium heat, stirring constantly. Reduce heat to low and continue cooking 1 minute, stirring constantly. Pour into the tart shell. Cool to room temperature and then refrigerate.

TOPPING

Beat the whipping cream in the bowl of a heavy-duty electric mixer with the whisk attachment

Finnish Blueberries
Vastavalo Mustikassa/VisitFinland.com

HELSINKI

With a population of over one million, Helsinki is the northernmost urban area in Europe. One in four Finns live there. Finland and Helsinki are known for bold architecture and clean modern lines. Because of the worldwide telecommunications giant Nokia, the population is also technologically advanced.

Helsinki was founded in 1550 by King Gustav I of Sweden but little came of it until the naval fortress Suomenlinna, sometimes called the "Gibraltar of the North," was built on an island across from the harbor. From 1788 to 1790 it was the base of operations for the Swedes in the Russo-Swedish War. In 1909 it was surrendered to Russia after a seige. The Russians chose to move the capital from Turku to Helsinki to be closer to Russia.

Carl Ludvig Engel was hired as the architect to design the city and was told to use St. Petersburg as a model. The oldest parts of the city a have a distinctive Russian feel with many fine neoclassic buildings.

until soft peaks form. Add the sugar and vanilla and continue beating until the sugar is dissolved. Spoon whipped cream onto the tart.

Rhubarb Custard Tart

Look for fresh tart, tangy rhubarb in late spring and early summer. Later in the season it can be especially tart. It grows well in cooler climates and usually disappears from the market in late summer. One pound of rhubarb yields about 3 cups. Select thin bright red stalks and remove the leaves just before using. Serve with whipped cream or ice cream.

SERVES 8

CRUST

1 1/4 cups	all-purpose flour		1/2 cup	unsalted butter, cold
2 tablespoons	sugar		1 tablespoon	distilled or cider vinegar
1/4 teaspoon	salt			

FILLING

1 cup	sugar		1	large egg, beaten
1/4 cup	all-purpose flour		3 cups	chopped fresh rhubarb
1/4 cup	heavy whipping cream			

TOPPING

3 tablespoons	all-purpose flour		2 tablespoons	unsalted butter
3 tablespoons	sugar			

Heat the oven to 375°F. Place the rack in the lower third of the oven. Lightly grease a 9-inch tart pan with a removeable bottom.

CRUST

Combine the flour, sugar, and salt for the crust in a food processor bowl. Add the cold butter and pulse until dough resembles coarse crumbs. With the processor running, add the vinegar. Process until dough starts to clump together, about 15 seconds.

Place the dough on a lightly floured surface and gather into a ball. Place the dough in center of the prepared tart pan. Using your fingers, press the dough out to the edges of the pan and all the way up the sides. Lightly dust your fingers with a little flour if dough is sticky.

FILLING

Combine the sugar and flour for the filling in a large bowl. Add the cream and egg and beat until smooth. Stir in the rhubarb. Spoon filling into the crust, distributing the fruit evenly.

TOPPING

Combine the topping ingredients in a small bowl and mix until coarse crumbs form. Sprinkle over the fruit.

Bake 45 minutes or until set in the center and the crust is golden brown. Cool on a wire cooling rack. Serve warm or chill until serving. Store this tart in the refrigerator.

The Crown Jewels at Rosenborg Castle
Ukendt / VisitDenmark.com

KING CHRISTIAN IV

King Christian IV built Rosenborg Castle in 1606 as a summer residence and it became his favorite residence. Located in the center of Copenhagen, it is where the Danish Crown Jewels are housed today. It is just one of the beautiful buildings he built in and around Copenhagen, including the Round Tower, the oldest functioning observatory in Europe, built in 1642. In addition, he founded new towns and strengthened ports.

Christian IV is one of the most popular of the Danish monarchs, having reigned for 60 years. During this time he fought to regain land captured by Sweden, reformed the government, and built many buildings that still stand. He joined the Thirty Years' War to protect Danish interests in northern Germany and defend the Lutheran faith. During a naval battle with Sweden he was hit with shrapnel and lost an eye. He continued fighting and inspiring his men, and his bravery is remembered in the Danish national anthem, "King Christian Stood by the Lofty Mast."

Country Style Pear Tart

D'Anjou pears or Bosc pears are the two varieties I find best for baking. D'Anjou are not available year round but Bosc are usually at the supermarket. Pears should be firm and just beginning to soften when pressed gently at the stem end. I usually allow pears several days at room temperature in a paper bag for proper ripening. Crisp unripe pears will usually soften when baked.

SERVES 8

CRUST

1 1/2 cups	all-purpose flour
1/2 teaspoon	salt

1/2 cup	cold unsalted butter, cut into 1/2-inch cubes
3 tablespoons	water

FILLING

1 (7 ounce)	package almond paste
2 tablespoons	sugar
2 tablespoons	unsalted butter, melted

1	large egg
2	firm ripe pears, peeled, cored and sliced
1 tablespoon	lemon juice

Heat the oven to 375°F. Place the rack in the lower third of the oven. Lightly grease a baking sheet.

CRUST

Combine the flour and salt in a food processor bowl. Add the cold butter and pulse until dough resembles coarse crumbs. With the processor running, add 3 tablespoons of water. Process until dough starts to clump together, about 15 seconds. If the dough doesn't begin to clump, add more water, 1 teaspoon at a time, until it does begin to clump.

Turn dough onto lightly floured surface and gather into a ball. Roll out to an 11-inch circle, keeping dough as round as possible. Loosely roll dough around rolling pin and lift onto center of a baking sheet.

FILLING

Place the almond paste in the bowl of a food processor and pulse until small pieces form. (You don't need to clean the bowl after making the crust.) Add sugar, butter and egg and process until smooth. Spread into an 8-inch circle on the pastry.

Gently toss the pear slices with the lemon juice to prevent browning. Arrange the pear slices over the almond filling by overlapping around the edge. Press together any cracks around the edges of the pastry. Fold about 1 1/2 inches of the pastry over the filling. It will not completely cover the fruit.

Bake 50 to 60 minutes or until the filling is set and the crust is golden brown. Cool on a wire cooling rack. Serve warm with ice cream, if desired.

Lumsass Mill
Kim Wyon/VisitDenmark.com

ALMOND PASTE

Almond is one of the most popular flavors in Scandinavia. Almond paste or marzipan is used in many classic cakes, cookies, pastries and breads. Almond paste and marzipan are both made with finely ground blanched almonds, sugar, egg whites, and corn syrup or glycerin. Almond paste is grainier and marzipan is smoother and more pliable. Almond extract is often added to enhance the flavor.

Almond paste can be purchased in cans or in a tightly sealed package in the baking aisle of most supermarkets. It should be firm and pliable but sometimes, it is too firm to crumble. When it is very firm, grate it with a box grater or chop finely using a food processor before adding it to your recipe. After opened, it must be very tightly wrapped before storing in the refrigerator.

Marzipan can be rolled to cover cakes, molded into fruit shapes, and can also be painted with food coloring for decorations. Marzipan must sometimes be purchased from specialty food stores.

Mazarin Tarts

These tender tarts are bursting with almond flavor. Decorate the tops by creating patterns with toasted almond slices. You'll need 3-inch tart pans for individual tarts. I prefer tart pans without removeable bottoms. Loosen edges gently with a wooden skewer before removing the tarts.

SERVES 8 (3-INCH TARTS)

CRUST

1 1/2 cups	all-purpose flour		1/2 cup	unsalted butter, cut into 1/2-inch cubes
3 tablespoons	sugar		1	large egg yolk
1/4 teaspoon	salt		1 tablespoon	cold water

FILLING

1 (7 oz) package	almond paste (See page 57)		2	large eggs
1/4 cup	sugar		1/2 teaspoon	pure almond extract
2 tablespoons	all-purpose flour			

FROSTING

1 1/2 cups	confectioners' sugar		Sliced almonds, toasted
2 to 3 tablespoons	2% milk		

Heat the oven to 350°F. Place the rack in the center of the oven.

CRUST

Combine the flour, sugar and salt for the crust in a food processor bowl. Add the cold butter and pulse until dough resembles coarse crumbs. Mix egg yolk and water. With the processor running, add the liquid. Process until dough starts to clump together, about 15 seconds.

Place the dough on a lightly floured surface and gather into a ball. Divide into 8 pieces. Press each piece into a 3-inch tart pan, pressing up sides. Place pans on a baking sheet.

FILLING

Combine the almond paste, sugar and 2 tablespoons flour in the food processor bowl. (You don't need to clean the bowl after making the crust.) Process until almost smooth, about 10 seconds. Add eggs and almond extract and process until mixed. Spoon the filling into pastry crusts, spreading evenly.

Bake 20 to 25 minutes or until golden brown. Remove from the baking sheet and cool tarts on wire cooling racks.

FROSTING

Beat confectioners' sugar and 2 tablespoons milk in a small bowl until smooth.

Vasa Warship, Built from 1626 to 1668
Yory Frenklakh/Shutterstock.com

THE VASA MUSEUM

The Vasa Museum, one of Europe's great historical experiences and Stockholm's most popular museum, opened in 1990. The museum was built to house the royal warship, Vasa, that capsized in Stockholm harbor 20 minutes into its maiden voyage in 1628. This pride of the navy was top heavy with more cannons than other ships of the same size and blew over in a strong wind. It lay undiscovered at the bottom of the harbor until 1956 when it was rediscovered by a marine biologist. The muddy waters of the harbor protected it from decay.

After nearly 50 years of careful preservation, this seventeenth century treasure has been restored to its former glory. The three masts are mounted on the top of the museum to illustrate their actual height on the ship. The figurehead is a 10-foot lion representing King Gustav II Adolph, who was known as the "Lion of the North." The sides of the ship were decorated with 500 carved statues that were painted in bright colors and are slowly being restored to their original brilliance.

Remove tarts from the pans by loosening sides and inverting. Spread tops with frosting and garnish with toasted almonds.

Lemon Mousse

Use fresh lemons for this light citrus dessert. Always wash lemons, oranges and limes before grating the peel. Although the peel is strained out of the curd, it adds a lot of flavor.

1 package (1/4 oz)	unflavored gelatin		3	large eggs, well beaten
1/4 cup	water		1 tablespoon	grated lemon peel
1 1/2 cups	sugar		1 cup	heavy whipping cream
3/4 cup	freshly squeezed lemon juice		2 tablespoons	sugar
6 tablespoons	cold unsalted butter, cut into 1/2-inch pieces			

Sprinkle the gelatin over the water in a small bowl and let stand about 5 minutes or until it absorbs the water.

Combine the sugar, lemon juice, butter, eggs and lemon peel in a small heavy saucepan and cook over medium-low heat, stirring constantly. The butter will be just melted when the curd thickens. Bring the mixture just to the point where some bubbles rise and the sauce has thickened, about 6 to 8 minutes. An instant-read thermometer should read 185°F. Use a silicone spatula for stirring, and cook until sauce coats the spatula. When you draw your finger across the back of the spatula, the path should remain. Remove from the heat and add the gelatin. Stir until the gelatin dissolves completely.

Strain into a large bowl and cover the surface with plastic wrap to prevent a skin from forming. Cool to room temperature. Refrigerate until lemon curd mounds when stirred, about 3 hours.

Beat the whipping cream in the bowl of a heavy-duty electric mixer with the whisk attachment until soft peaks form. Beat in sugar on low until dissolved. Add about 1/4 of the whipped cream to the lemon curd and stir until blended. Fold in remaining whipped cream and spoon into individual serving dishes. Chill until set, about 2 hours.

Sotasæter, Breheimen
Anders Gjengedal/VisitNorway.com

HOW TO FOLD

Folding is an important step in baking and is used to combine a light airy mixture with a heavier mixture without deflating either. Be sure to use a large bowl for the heavier mixture so there is enough room for the motion. Start by placing about 1/4 of the lighter mixture (usually egg whites or whipped cream) on top of the heavier mixture, stirring until blended. By lightening the heavier mixture, it is easier to add the second mixture without over-mixing.

A rubber spatula is the best utensil to use for folding. Begin by holding the spatula vertically and cutting down to the bottom of the bowl in the center. Pull the spatula horizontally across the bottom of the bowl toward the back, combining the two mixtures. Turn the bowl a quarter turn and repeat the process. By cutting down, across, up and over, the light airy mixture isn't deflated. Continue the folding motion until the 2 mixtures are just blended. This technique is used in cakes leavened by air, such as sponge cakes, soufflés and meringues.

Hazelnut Meringue with Raspberries

This is an easy summer dessert with which you can use a variety of fresh fruits including strawberries, peaches, nectarines and kiwi fruit. Meringues should be placed in air-tight containers and stored at room temperature (but don't bake the meringues on a humid day). Remove the bitter skins from the hazelnuts for the best flavor.

SERVES 8

4	large egg whites, room temperature
1/2 teaspoon	cream of tartar
1 cup	superfine sugar
1/2 cup	ground toasted hazelnuts
1 teaspoon	vanilla
1 cup	heavy whipping cream
2 pints	fresh raspberries

Heat the oven to 300°F. Line two baking sheets with parchment paper and draw four 4- to 5-inch circles on each sheet by tracing around a small plate. Place drawing-side down on the baking sheets.

For the meringue, beat the egg whites in a large bowl on medium speed until frothy, using the whisk attachment. Beat in the cream of tartar and beat on medium until soft peaks form. Gradually add the sugar, 1 tablespoon at a time, beating on high speed until the sugar is dissolved and the meringue holds stiff glossy peaks when the beater is lifted, 4 to 6 minutes. (See page 25, "Baking with Eggs," for special tips on making a meringue.) Fold in the hazelnuts and vanilla.

Spoon the meringue onto the circles on the parchment and spread to the edges using a metal spatula, mounding slightly higher around the edges. Place in the oven and reduce the temperature to 250°F. Bake for 30 to 40 minutes or until firm and dry to the touch. Any cracks may look slightly moist. Remove and cool completely on a wire cooling rack. When cool, carefully peel off the paper. (I find cutting the paper about 1/2 inch from the meringues makes it easier to remove without breaking the shells.)

Beat the whipping cream in the bowl of a heavy-duty electric mixer with the whisk attachment on high speed until soft peaks form. Spread whipped cream into the center of each meringue and garnish with raspberries. Chill until serving.

BAKER'S TIP: To use granulated sugar in place of superfine sugar, place 1 cup + 1 teaspoon granulated sugar in a food processor. Process several seconds until the sugar is finely ground.

A Goat Grazing a Meadow in Finland
Anneli Honisto/VisitFinland.com

HAZELNUTS

Hazelnuts grow in clusters on bushes found abundantly throughout Europe are popular in Scandinavian baking. Sometimes they're called filberts because they ripen around August 22, the feast of St. Philbert.

They are covered with a bitter skin that should be removed. Occasionally, you can find chopped filberts that have already had the skin removed. The easiest way to remove the skins is by baking. Place hazelnuts on a baking sheet and bake about 12 to 15 minutes in a 350°F oven until the skins split. After removing them from the oven, wrap the nuts is a clean dishtowel and let them cool. This traps the steam, loosening the skins. Using the towel, rub the nuts vigorously until most of the skins are removed. I find it difficult to remove every trace of the skins, but small amounts don't affect the flavor.

Hazelnuts are high is fiber and carbohydrates, iron, calcium and Vitamin E. They also contain healthy mono-unsaturated fats.

Danish Aeblekage

There are lots of versions of this traditional favorite that is sometimes called "Peasant Girl with a Veil." Homemade applesauce has great flavor and lots of texture but many cooks prefer thick, canned applesauce. For one of my friends, this is a Christmas Eve tradition passed down through several generations.

SERVES 8 TO 10

3 pounds	cooking apples, peeled, cored and chopped
1/2 cup	firmly packed brown sugar
1 tablespoon	lemon juice
3 tablespoons	water
1/4 cup	sugar
1/4 cup	unsalted butter
2 cups	fine dry bread crumbs (rusk)
1/2 cup	heavy whipping cream
1 tablespoon	sugar
1/2 teaspoon	vanilla
	Fresh raspberries, currant jelly or raspberry jam

Combine the apples, brown sugar, lemon juice and water in a large saucepan or Dutch oven. Cover and bring to a boil over medium heat, stirring occasionally. Reduce heat to low and cook until apples are tender and juices have evaporated, about 40 minutes. Cool to room temperature.

Melt the butter in a large skillet over low heat and add the breadcrumbs and sugar. Cook over low heat, stirring constantly, until golden brown and caramelized, about 7 to 10 minutes. Cool to room temperature.

Butter a 2-quart bowl. Spread a layer of applesauce in the bottom of the bowl. Top with crumbs. Alternate layers until all crumbs and applesauce are used. Press firmly to compact layers. Cover and chill overnight.

Loosen dessert from sides of the bowl and invert onto a serving plate. Beat the whipping cream in the bowl of a heavy-duty electric mixer, with the whisk attachment, on high speed until soft peaks form. Add the sugar and vanilla and beat on low until sugar is dissolved.

Decorate with whipped cream. Garnish as desired with raspberries, currant jelly or raspberry jam.

BAKER'S TIP: Use a coarse or chewy bread like French bread to make the crumbs. This dessert can also be layered in a trifle bowl, clear glass bowl or individual serving cups.

Childhood Home of Hans Christian Andersen in Odense
Lennard Nielsen/VisitDenmark.com

HANS CHRISTIAN ANDERSEN

Hans Christian Andersen is recognized all over the world for his children's fairy tales including "The Little Mermaid," "The Ugly Duckling" and "The Little Match Girl." His works have been translated into more than 150 languages and made into movies, animated films, plays and ballets.

He was born in 1805 in Odense, Denmark, the only child of a shoemaker and his wife. He was 11 when his father died and he was forced into manual labor as a weaver's apprentice and later as a tailor. At the age of 14, he moved to Copenhagen to become an actor and became a member of the Royal Theatre as a boy soprano. Unfortunately, when his voice changed, he was forced to leave. His director encouraged him to return to school.

He considered himself a misfit, which is a topic reflected in many of his works, such as "The Ugly Duckling."

In 1904, to celebrate his 100th birthday, the city of Odense founded a museum in his childhood home. In addition to his fairy tales, loved by both children and adults, he published novels, poetry and travelogues. By the end of his life, he was cultured, wealthy and had been knighted. He died in Copenhagen in 1875. The statue of "The Little Mermaid" was erected in 1909 as a gift to the city of Copenhagen and is one of its most recognized sights.

Cardamom Rusks

Swedish Almond Bars

Raspberry Shortbread

Buttery Swedish Spritz

Tosca Mini-Tarts

Cinnamon Sugar Twists

Norwegian Kringla

COOKIES & BARS

COOKIES AND BARS ARE POPULAR WITH BAKERS BECAUSE THEY ARE EASY TO MAKE, require little time and few ingredients, and fill the home with enticing scents. Butter, sugar, flour, eggs, baking powder or baking soda are often the only ingredients required. When nuts are added, toasting enhances their nutty flavor. Almonds are used most often in Scandinavian baking but you can substitute walnuts or pecans.

Swedish Almond Bars have a rich buttery topping and a shortbread crust. Cinnamon Sugar Twists are made using a technique similar to creating Danish pastry but have a crackly crystallized coating. Meeting friends for coffee is a Scandinavian tradition and twice-baked rusk, redolent with cardamom, are a familiar accompaniment to steaming cups of coffee.

Butter is the fat I prefer for cookies because it has outstanding flavor and makes cookies easy to shape or roll. Most cookie recipes call for softened butter—butter that is still firm but holds an imprint when pressed with a finger. If you use butter, allow it to stand at room temperature for about 30 minutes or in microwave on defrost for 10 to 15 seconds. When cookie dough becomes too soft, cookies can spread too much, but this is easily remedied by chilling the dough. Even though you may be tempted, don't add extra flour or the cookies will be dry.

Bake the cookies on ungreased cookie sheets unless the recipe directs otherwise. Because cookies can go from delicately browned to hard and dark quickly, I recommend checking for doneness about one minute early. You can always add another minute or two for golden brown edges. Always cool cookies on cooling racks to maintain their crisp texture. Most cookies are best when stored at room temperature.

Cardamom Rusks

Rusks are popular accompaniments, especially when they are fragrant with cardamom. These are shaped into logs before baking, but rusk can also be baked in a pan and sliced horizontally before toasting. For the best flavor, use freshly ground cardamom.

MAKES 3 DOZEN RUSKS

3 1/2 cups	all-purpose flour
1 teaspoon	baking powder
1 1/2 teaspoons	ground cardamom
1/4 teaspoon	salt
1/2 cup	sugar
1/2 cup	firmly-packed brown sugar
3/4 cup	unsalted butter, softened
2	large eggs, beaten
3/4 cup	chopped toasted hazelnuts
1	egg white, beaten
	Swedish pearl sugar

Heat the oven to 350°F. Line two baking sheets with parchment paper or grease thoroughly. Combine the flour, baking powder, cardamom and salt in a medium bowl.

Beat the sugar, brown sugar and butter in a large bowl with an electric mixer on medium speed until creamy. Beat in the eggs. With mixer on low speed, gradually add the flour mixture and beat until dough forms. Stir in the hazelnuts.

Divide the dough into 2 parts. Shape each half into a log about 12 inches long and 2 1/2 to 3 inches wide. Place one log on each baking sheet. Flatten slightly to about 1/2-inch thickness. Brush tops with egg white and sprinkle with pearl sugar.

Bake 25 to 30 minutes or until lightly browned and firm to the touch. Remove from the oven and cool slightly on the baking sheet.

Cut each log into diagonal slices about 3/4-inch thick, using a serrated knife or a bread knife. Place slices flat on baking sheet and return to the oven. Bake 8 to 10 minutes or until toasted. Turn slices over and continue baking, 8 to 10 minutes or until second side is toasted. Cool on a wire cooling rack.

Store in an air-tight container.

Helsinki Hakaniemi Market Hall
VisitFinland.com

HOW TO STORE AND SHIP COOKIES

Because most cookie recipes make several dozen it is important to know how to store the cookies to keep them at their best. Cool cookies completely before storing and make sure that icing or frosting is dry and set. Don't combine crisp cookies in the same container as soft cookies or the texture of both will change. Store most cookies at room temperature but refrigerate cookies or bars with cream cheese or custard fillings. Strong flavored cookies such as Ginger Snaps should be stored in separate containers or mild cookies will pick up the spicy flavor. Most cookies and bars will keep well 3 to 5 days at room temperature. For longer storage, wrap tightly and freeze. Place a piece of waxed paper between layers. Unwrap cookies and thaw at room temperature.

Especially during the holidays, many bakers want to ship cookies. Cookies and bars ship well in general. Don't try to ship cookies or bars that need to be refrigerated. If you want to send chewy cookies, consider shipping priority to preserve their freshness, as they can easily dry out. Pack cookies is a sturdy tin or plastic container and don't crowd them. Sometime I wrap a stack of 4 or 5 together and then place them in the shipping container. Surround the tin with packing peanuts or popcorn (for an added treat!). When you've taken the time to bake, it makes sense to ship the gift quickly so they arrive in peak condition.

Swedish Almond Bars

MAKES 3 DOZEN

COOKIES

2 cups	all-purpose flour		1/4 teaspoon	salt
1 1/2 cups	confectioners' sugar		3/4 cup	unsalted butter, cold

TOPPING

1/2 cup	firmly packed brown sugar		1/4 cup	unsalted butter, melted
2 tablespoons	all-purpose flour		1 cup	sliced almonds, toasted
1/4 cup	heavy whipping cream			

Combine the flour, confectioners' sugar and salt for the crust in a medium bowl. Cut in the butter with a pastry blender until mixture resembles coarse crumbs. Press the dough into an ungreased 13 x 9-inch baking pan. Bake 15 to 18 minutes or until the edges begin to brown.

Mix the brown sugar and 2 tablespoons flour in a small saucepan. Add the whipping cream and butter and mix well. Cook over medium heat until the mixture comes to a boil. Reduce the heat to low and cook until thickened, stirring constantly. Remove the pan from the heat and stir in the almonds. Pour over the warm crust.

Bake 10 to 14 minutes or until the topping is bubbling. Place the pan on a wire rack and run a spatula around the edge to release bars. Cool on a wire cooling rack. Cut into bars.

Raspberry Shortbread

MAKES 5 TO 6 DOZEN BARS

BARS

2 cups	all-purpose flour		1 cup	unsalted butter, cut into cubes
1/2 cup	confectioners' sugar		1/2 cup	raspberry jam
1/4 teaspoon	salt			

GLAZE

1 cup	confectioners' sugar		1 teaspoon	pure almond extract
2 to 3 teaspoons	milk			

Heat the oven to 350°F. Stagger the oven racks.

Beat the flour, sugar, salt and butter in a large bowl until dough forms. Divide the dough into thirds.

Press each 1/3 of the dough into a strip no wider than 2 inches and about 3/8-inch thick on an ungreased baking sheet. Place 2 strips on a baking sheet. Press a slight indentation down the center, the length of each strip. Fill the indentation with jam.

Bake 15 to 18 minutes or until edges are lightly browned. Rotate baking pans as needed for even browning. Cool on a wire cooling rack.

Beat confectioners' sugar, 2 teaspoons milk and almond extract in a small bowl for the glaze. Add milk if necessary to make a thin glaze. Drizzle the glaze over the bars and cut the bars into 1-inch slices. Store in a loosely covered container.

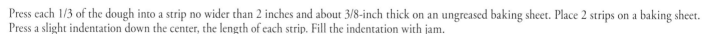

Buttery Swedish Spritz

MAKES 4 TO 5 DOZEN COOKIES

3/4 cup	sugar		1 teaspoon	vanilla
1 cup	unsalted butter, softened		1/4 teaspoon	salt
1	large egg		2 cups	all-purpose flour

Heat the oven to 375°F. Place the oven rack in the center of the oven.

Beat the sugar and butter in the bowl of a heavy-duty mixer on medium speed until creamy. Add the egg, vanilla and salt and beat until mixed well, scraping down the sides of the bowl. Add the flour and beat on low until dough forms. Color dough, if desired.

Fit a disk on a cookie press and fill the press with dough. Form cookies on ungreased baking sheets about 1 inch apart. Chill remaining dough until needed. Decorate with sprinkles or colored sugar, if desired. If your dough becomes too firm with chilling, allow it to warm briefly at room temperature.

Bake cookies 10 to 12 minutes or until edges just begin to brown. Cool on baking sheet 1 minute and remove. Cool completely on a wire cooling rack.

Tosca Mini-Tarts

MAKES 24 TARTS

TARTS

1 1/2 cups	all-purpose flour		1/2 cup	cold unsalted butter, cut into 1/2-inch cubes
1/4 cup	sugar			
1/4 teaspoon	salt		3 tablespoons	sour cream

FILLING

1 can (7 ounces)	almond paste		1	large egg, beaten
1/4 cup	sugar		1/4 cup	sliced almonds, toasted
2 tablespoons	heavy whipping cream			

Heat the oven to 375°F. Place the oven rack in the center of the oven.

Pulse the flour, sugar, salt and butter in a food processor bowl until mixture resembles coarse crumbs. Add the sour cream and process until dough forms, 20 to 30 seconds. Place the dough on a lightly floured surface and shape into a ball. Divide into 24 pieces. Press into 24 cups in ungreased mini-muffin pans. Dip your thumb or finger in flour if it begins to stick to the dough.

Combine the almond paste and sugar in a food processor bowl and pulse until mixture resembles coarse crumbs. Add the whipping cream and egg and process briefly until mixed. Divide the filling into the pastry-lined cups, filling about 3/4 full. Use about 2 teaspoons of filling per cup. Top each with a few almond slices.

Bake 15 to 18 minutes or until golden brown. Cool on wire cooling racks for 5 minutes. Remove from pans and cool completely. (I use a thin metal spatula to loosen the tarts. Carefully insert the spatula on a side and gently lift the tart.) Store loosely covered at room temperature.

Cinnamon Sugar Twists

Because this dough is folded several times, its tender buttery layers shatter in your mouth at the first bite. I always shape up the dough to the correct dimensions before starting the turns because it will be easier to maintain the shape as you fold and roll. When preparing anything with yeast, the most important step is to measure the temperature of the water. If the water is too hot, it will kill the yeast and your dough won't rise.

MAKES **64** TWISTS

1 (1/4 oz) package	active dry yeast	1/2 cup	sour cream
1/4 cup	warm water (105° to 115°F)	1 teaspoon	vanilla
4 cups	all-purpose flour	2	large eggs, well beaten
1 teaspoon	salt	1 cup	sugar
1 cup	cold unsalted butter, cut into 1/2-inch pieces	1 1/2 teaspoons	cinnamon

Sprinkle the yeast over the warm water and let stand 5 minutes until the yeast is dissolved. Combine the flour and salt in a large bowl. Cut in the butter on medium speed until mixture resembles coarse crumbs. You can also cut in the butter using a pastry blender.

Combine the sour cream, vanilla and eggs in a small bowl. Add to the flour and mix on low speed until soft dough forms. Place dough on a lightly floured surface, shape into a ball and divide in half. Wrap in waxed paper or plastic wrap. Chill at least 4 hours or overnight.

Heat the oven to 350°F. Place the oven rack in the center of the oven.

Combine sugar and cinnamon in a small bowl and sprinkle about 1/2 into a rectangle on a clean surface. Place 1/2 of the chilled dough over the sugar. Roll into a 16 x 8-inch rectangle, turning once to coat both sides with sugar. If the dough is too firm to roll, allow to stand at room temperature to soften, 15 to 30 minutes. If necessary, trim the dough and patch to form a rectangle. When rolling the dough, use a light touch so the dough doesn't become tough.

Fold 1/3 of the dough toward the center and fold the other end over, forming 3 layers. Turn the direction of the dough 1/4 turn and roll to a 16 x 8-inch rectangle again. Sprinkle with cinnamon sugar. Fold over 1/3 of the dough and cover with the final 1/3. Repeat the turning and folding and sprinkling with sugar. You are folding 3 times to form many layers. Allow to rest if the dough becomes too elastic to roll.

Roll dough to 16 x 8-inches and cut into 1-inch strips. Cut each strip in 1/2 forming 32 strips. Twist strips 2 or 3 times and place on an ungreased baking sheet. I press both ends of strip to the baking sheet to hold the twisted shape.

Repeat with the remaining 1/2 of dough. Bake 15 to 20 minutes or until golden brown. Cool on wire cooling racks. Store loosely covered at room temperature.

Old Horse and Carriage on a Farm in Oslo
Nancy Bundt/VisitNorway.com

LEIF ERICSON

Leif Ericson, son of Eric the Red, is credited with being the first European to set foot on the shores of North America almost 500 years before Columbus. His father, Eric Thorvaldsson, was exiled from Iceland and sailed with his family to form the first Norse colonies in Greenland, which is where Leif is thought to have grown up.

Icelandic sagas of the 13th century tell of the voyage of Leif Ericson around the year 1000 to lands west of Greenland, possibly following reports from Icelandic merchant Bjarni Herjolfsson of land he sighted west of Greenland after his ship was blown off course. Although it is not possible to know for sure, it is thought that he landed twice, once at what may be Baffin Island and again in Labrador, before establishing a colony that he named Vinland. There was no long-term permanent colony built due to poor relations with the local inhabitants.

Archeological exploration has uncovered a Viking site in North American at L'Anse aux Meadows at the northern tip of Newfoundland. At this site, archeologists discovered a longhouse with a great hall in the Viking style. Artifacts from the site include a soapstone spindle that indicates women may have been among the inhabitants.

In 1964, President Lyndon Johnson proclaimed "Leif Ericson Day."

Norwegian Kringla

Norwegian Kringla makes a perfect accompaniment to a steaming cup of coffee or warm cocoa. Spread the top lightly with rich creamery butter or honey for a treat. "Kringla" is the word for eight in Norwegian, the traditional shape of these cake-like cookies. The dough can also be rolled into pretzel shapes, which I find it a little easier.

MAKES 6 TO 7 DOZEN

6 cups	all-purpose flour
2 teaspoons	baking soda
1/2 teaspoon	salt
1 1/2 cups	sugar
3/4 cup	unsalted butter, softened

2	large eggs
1 teaspoon	vanilla
1 cup	low-fat buttermilk
1 cup	sour cream

Combine the flour, baking soda and salt in a medium bowl.

Beat the sugar and butter in the bowl of a heavy-duty mixer on medium speed until creamy. Add the eggs and vanilla and beat until mixed well, scraping down the sides of the bowl. With the mixer on low speed, add the buttermilk and sour cream and beat until blended. Slowly add the flour mixture and beat on low until dough forms. Place the dough on a lightly floured surface and shape into a ball. Wrap with waxed paper or plastic wrap and chill at least 2 hours.

Heat the oven to 400°F. Place the oven rack in the center of the oven. Line baking sheets with parchment paper or grease lightly.

Roll rounded tablespoonfuls of dough on well-floured surface into pencil shapes about 8 inches long. Shape into pretzel shapes or figure 8s and place on baking sheets. Bake 8 to 10 minutes. Cool on wire cooling racks.

Store at room temperature in a tightly sealed container.

BAKER'S TIP: Before baking, you can brush cookies with milk and sprinkle with Swedish pearl sugar.

Nidarosdomen Cathedral
Christoffer Hansen Vika/Shutterstock.com

NIDAROSDOMEN CATHEDRAL

Nidarosdomen Cathedral, Norway's National Cathedral, is located in Trondheim and was built over the site where St. Olav was buried. King Olav Haraldsson was killed in battle in 1030 and secretly buried by the river Nid. His gravesite remained a secret for a year, marked by a small chapel that was built there. One year and 5 days after his death, he was declared a saint. Tradition has it that the main altar is built over his grave.

Construction of the cathedral at the site began in 1070 and finished around 1300. This was typical for churches build in the Middle Ages where such construction took hundreds of years. At that time, it was the most beautiful church in Norway. It was destroyed several times by fire and rebuilt each time, mainly in the Gothic style. Beautiful stained glass windows were installed in the twentieth century.

Nidarosdomen Cathedral was an important destination for pilgrims until the Reformation and currently receives about 400,000 visitors a year,. Today it is the largest remaining medieval building in Scandinavia.

Riding the Beaches of Iceland
Mark Vest/VisitIceland.com

TRADITIONAL FAVORITES

CELEBRATIONS THROUGHOUT THE WORLD OFTEN INCLUDE SPECIAL FOODS and rituals as a part of the festivities. Celebrating Christmas with family and friends is an age-old tradition, especially in Scandinavia where the winters are cold and dark. Many of the traditional favorites found in Scandinavian homes during the Christmas season are baked in special utensils and pans that have been passed down from mother to daughter. They also can be purchased in specialty stores and through the internet. (See Sources, page 96). Delicate and buttery, Krumkake are baked in a krumkake iron and shaped around a wooden cone while they are warm, forming cornucopias that can be filled with whipped cream. Rosettes are fried and come in many shapes, traditionally finished by a delicate dusting of confectioners' sugar. Both of these are found in many homes and probably made only once a year because they are time consuming to make. Golden brown round pancake balls, Aebleskiver, are a traditional Christmas morning breakfast treat in Denmark but also favorites throughout the year.

Swedish Princess Cake and Norwegian Kransekake are often the centerpiece for many Scandinavian celebrations. Because they are elaborate and require many hours to complete, they're usually purchased from bakeries. I included the recipes here for anyone with the time for preparing something unique for that special occasion.

Follow the carefully written directions for these specialties and adopt one or several for your family celebrations, honoring old traditions or creating new ones. As with all baking, these techniques become easier with practice.

Danish Aebleskiver

Traditional Danish aebleskiver usually has a little applesauce in the center. You can use a thick applesauce or use the filling I've included below. I like using golden delicious or gala apples. Choose your favorite cooking apple and cook until apples are tender and any juices have thickened.

MAKES 4 DOZEN

1/3 cup	unsalted butter
1/3 cup	firmly packed brown sugar
2 1/2 to 3 cups	finely chopped, cored, peeled apples (2 to 3 medium apples)
1 teaspoon	cinnamon
1 (1/4 oz) package	active dry yeast
1/4 cup	warm water (105° to 115°F)

3	large eggs, separated
2 tablespoons	sugar
2 cups	all-purpose flour
1/2 teaspoon	salt
1 1/4 cups	2% milk
1 teaspoon	vanilla
1/4 cup	unsalted butter, melted
	Cinnamon sugar

Melt the butter with the brown sugar in a 9-inch skillet. Add the apples and cinnamon and cook over medium heat about 5 to 8 minutes, stirring often, until the apples are tender and liquid has evaporated. Cool to room temperature.

Sprinkle the yeast over the warm water and let stand 5 minutes until the yeast is dissolved.

Whisk the egg yolks and sugar in a medium bowl until foamy. Combine the flour and salt in a medium bowl. Add the flour mixture, 1/2 cup milk and vanilla to the egg yolks and whisk until smooth. Beat in the remaining milk.

Beat the egg whites in a large bowl with the electric mixer on high speed until soft peaks form. When you lift the beaters, the whites will make peaks that fold back slightly.

Gently fold the egg whites into the batter until smooth. (See "How to Fold," page 61). Let stand at room temperature 30 to 45 minutes until very light.

Heat an aebleskiver pan over medium heat until drops of water sizzle and bounce around. Brush each cup with melted butter. Add about 1 tablespoon batter to each cup. Top with a rounded 1/2 teaspoon apple filling and another tablespoon batter. Each cup should be almost full. Cook 1 to 2 minutes or until bottom half is browned. Using a knitting needle or wooden skewer, slowly turn balls to cook the other sides. Balls are done when a toothpick inserted in the center comes out clean.

Turn out pancake balls onto a plate and keep warm in a slow oven (200°F). Dust with cinnamon sugar. Pancakes are served warm but the filling can be very hot.

BAKER'S TIP: Substitute chunky applesauce for the cinnamon apples.

Råbjerg Mile, Jutland
VisitFinland.com

JUTLAND

The Danish mainland lies on the peninsula of Jutland that extends north from Europe. Jutland is bordered on the east by the North Sea and the west by the Baltic. It is this peninsula where Denmark shares a border with Germany and connects Denmark to the rest of Europe. The German provinces of Schleiswig and Holstein also share the peninsula. This land is filled with sand dunes, heaths, plains, peat bogs and ancient manor houses. It is also the location of one of the most popular attractions in Scandinavia, Legoland. Lego began in the workshop of a carpenter in 1932 where he created wooden toys that he named "leg godt" which means "play well." Legoland is filled with rides, restaurants, trees and legos. The 30 million legos are arranged into familiar shapes, including entire countries, and familiar landmarks such as Mount Rushmore, the Pantheon, Mad Ludwig's Castle and the Statue of Liberty.

Traphold Musuem for Modern Kunst (Modern Art, Applied Art, Design and Furniture Design) is also located in Jutland along the banks of the Kolding Fjord. In addition to twentieth century art, it houses the Danish Furniture Museum with its display of Danish chairs, providing an historical overview of popular Danish modern furniture.

Orange Aebleskiver with Chocolate Sauce

Orange peel and orange juice bring lots of delicate citrus flavor to these pancake balls. Chocolate sauce and maybe some whipped cream, dress this pancake up for dinner or dessert. I also like the orange flavor with lots of powdered sugar. It takes a little practice to make the round balls, but these puffs will become a family favorite no matter their shape!

MAKES 3 ½ DOZEN

2 cups	all-purpose flour		1/2 cup	orange juice
1 teaspoon	baking powder		1 teaspoon	vanilla
1/2 teaspoon	salt		1 tablespoon	grated orange peel
4	large eggs, separated		1/4 cup	butter, melted
2 tablespoons	sugar			Chocolate sauce
1 1/2 cups	2% milk			

Combine the flour, baking powder and salt in a small bowl. In a large bowl, whisk the egg yolks and sugar until foamy. Add the flour mixture and beat until smooth. Slowly beat in the milk, orange juice and vanilla and whisk until smooth. Stir in the grated orange peel.

Beat the egg whites in a large bowl with the electric mixer on high speed until soft peaks form. When you lift the beaters, the whites will make peaks that fold back slightly.

Gently fold the egg whites into the batter until smooth. (See "Baking with Eggs," page 25.)

Heat an aebleskiver pan over medium heat until drops of water sizzle and bounce around. Brush each cup with melted butter. Add about 1/4 cup batter to each cup, filling about 3/4 full. Cook 1 to 2 minutes or until bottom half is browned. Using a knitting needle or wooden skewer, slowly turn balls to cook the other sides. Balls are done when a wooden pick inserted in the center comes out clean.

Turn out pancake balls onto plate and keep warm in a slow oven (200°F). Drizzle with chocolate sauce and serve warm.

A Houseboat in Copenhagen
Kim Wyon/VisitDenmark.com

COPENHAGEN

One of Europe's oldest capitals, Copenhagen, is built on two main islands, Zealand and Amager, and is a vibrant city surrounded by water and connected by canals and bridges. Tour the city on a canal boat cruise or borrow a free bike and travel like the Danes do. Copenhagen is recognized for its high quality of life and attention to the environment. With the completion of the Oresund Bridge connecting it to Sweden, it is the center of a growing economic area.

Stroget is the world's longest pedestrian shopping area and includes some of the most exclusive and expensive brands in the world. Beginning at City Hall, several of Copenhagan's most beautiful sites are also along its length including the Cathedral of Our Lady and Gammeltorv, Tivoli Garden and Christianhavn in the old town center. The public library, the Black Diamond, overlooks the harbor and is a supermodern building made of black granite. It reflects the cutting edge design visible all over Denmark. Contrast the library with the Round Tower that was built by Christian IV in 1642 as an observatory and is still functioning.

Visited by millions each year, Tivoli Garden is one of the world's most famous amusement parks, a green oasis twinkling with lights from over 100,000 lanterns.

Swedish Glogg

Swedish immigrants brought this traditional hot red wine punch to the United States. In Sweden, no holiday celebration is complete without a steaming pan or punch bowl of this spicy hot punch. Place spoons in the cups to eat the wine-soaked fruit and nuts.

SERVES 8 TO 10

1 1/2 cups	water		1	peel of orange
1/2 cup	sugar		2 bottles (750 ml)	red wine
1 tablespoon	cardamom pods, crushed		1/2 cup	aquavit, optional
1 teaspoon	whole cloves		1 cup	raisins
2	cinnamon sticks		1 cup	slivered almonds

Combine the water, sugar, cardamom, cloves, cinnamon sticks and orange peel in a small saucepan and bring to a boil. Reduce heat to low and simmer 30 minutes. Strain through a strainer, reserving the liquid. Discard the spices. This can be done several days ahead and refrigerated.

Place the wine in a 5-quart Dutch oven and add the reserved liquid. Cook over low heat until liquid begins to simmer. Simmer 10 minutes. Add the aquavit, raisins and almonds and simmer 5 minutes. Cool slightly and serve in punch bowl or ladle directly into cups.

Serve in heat-proof cups or glasses. Add raisins and almonds to each serving.

Church Village of Gammelstad, Lulea, Sweden
irakite/Shutterstock.com

CHRISTMAS TRADITIONS

In December the days are short and the nights long and dark because of Scandinavia's location in northern Europe. To brighten the days candles are used extensively and twinkling lights are placed outdoors and reflect snow and ice crystals. Scandinavian homes are always prepared for unexpected visitors, especially during the holidays. Holiday preparations begin early in December and last through Twelfth Night or January 13, St. Knut's Day. The house is cleaned, baking begins and candles are purchased anticipating many guests and gatherings. Traditions overlap among the Scandinavian countries with food and folklore. One tradition holds that the Christmas spirit can't be allowed to leave the house so all guests are offered something to eat before they depart. This is one reason cookie recipes often make 8 or 10 dozen. Christmas meals vary in the different countries but almost everywhere Rice Pudding with a hidden almond is the traditional dessert and the person who finds the almond wins a prize.

In Sweden, the Jultomte hands out gifts to children. In Denmark and Norway, nisse protect the farm or home and a bowl of rice pudding is left out to keep them happy so they don't cause mischief. Traditions from pagan times and Christian rituals entwine for festivities throughout the season.

MoMo's Swedish Plette

Serve these delicate lacy pancakes with lingonberries, fruit preserves or syrup. I like them sprinkled with confectioners' sugar. These pancakes bake in a Swedish 5- or 7-section pancake pan, making 3-inch pancakes. You can also make 3-inch pancakes on a non-stick griddle using about 2 teaspoons batter per pancake.

SERVES 6 TO 8

3	large eggs, room temperature	2 cups	2% milk
1/3 cup	sugar	1/3 cup	unsalted butter, melted and cooled
1/2 teaspoon	salt		Melted butter
1 cup	all-purpose flour		Lingonberry preserves

Have the ingredients at room temperature. Using a whisk, beat the eggs, sugar and salt in a medium bowl until light. Add the flour and beat until smooth. Slowly beat in the milk. Stir in the melted butter.

Heat the pancake pan over medium-high heat until drops of water sizzle and bounce around when dropped onto the pan. Place scant 1 tablespoon batter in each cup and cook about 1 minute until dry on the surface and the edges begin to brown. Using a thin metal spatula, turn the pancakes. Continue cooking about 30 seconds until the second side is browned. Serve at once or keep warm in a 200°F oven until ready to serve.

Serve with lingonberry preserves or maple syrup or dust with confectioners' sugar.

A Norse Viking Ship Sailing at Sea
Paul B. Moore/Shutterstock.com

VIKINGS

Warm welcomes and Scandinavian hospitality have a long history in the Nordic countries. Many shared customs and traditions can be traced back to the Vikings. Although best known for their ferocious pillaging, hospitable Vikings in this rugged land welcomed unexpected guests.

The word "Viking" comes from the Swedish word "vik" meaning fjord or inlet; the Vikings were the scourge of the seas in the ninth and tenth centuries. Because of the inhospitable lands of Scandinavia, most settlements were along the coastlines. With lumber from nearby forests and impressive boatbuilding skills, the Vikings built longships with flat-bottomed hulls, perfect for the shallow waters along the coasts. The ships were powered by wind and oarsmen; they were stealthy, could appear suddenly and land directly on beaches. As warriors came charging off the ships, it's easy to understand how they brought terror to local inhabitants.

Danes and Norwegians traveled east to Greenland, England and Ireland, as the Swedes sailed west to Constantinople and along the Russian rivers. Scandinavians founded Dublin, settled Normandy, colonized Iceland and eventually colonized Greenland. These voyages were often looking for trade but could become violent when commerce proved impossible.

Rosettes

No festive holiday table in Scandinavia is complete without rosettes. These cookies are shaped using a rosette iron and fried in hot oil, shortening or lard. The most traditional shape is a delicate round but there are several other shapes that can be attached to the handle. The secret to success is to maintain the oil at the correct temperature.

MAKES 3 DOZEN COOKIES

2	large eggs, room temperature	1 cup	all-purpose flour
2 tablespoons	sugar	1 cup	whole or 2% milk
1/4 teaspoon	salt	1 1/2 quarts	vegetable oil (48 ounces)
1 teaspoon	vanilla		Confectioners' sugar

Combine the eggs, sugar, salt and vanilla in a medium bowl and beat until well blended. Add the flour and beat until smooth. Slowly beat in the milk.

Place the oil in a large deep fat fryer or electric frying pan and heat to 375°F. (You can use a saucepan or sauté pan but it is hard to control the temperature. You will need a frying thermometer to measure the temperature accurately.) Attach the rosette iron to the handle and heat in the oil for about 2 minutes. Remove the iron and allow excess oil to drip into the pan.

Dip the hot iron into the batter leaving about 1/4 inch bare at the top. Place the iron into the hot oil and cook until golden brown, about 20 to 30 seconds. (Don't allow the iron to touch the bottom of the pan.) Lift the iron and allow the oil to drip back into the pan. Gently remove the cookie from the iron. Using care, place the hot cookie, hollow side down, onto paper towels.

Continue making cookies using all the batter. Dip the rosette iron into the oil and heat about 10 seconds before making each cookie. Check the temperature of the oil occasionally and try to keep it at 375°F. When the cookies are cool, sprinkle with confectioners' sugar.

These cookies are best the day that they are made but will keep 2 days at room temperature. Store in an airtight container and use waxed paper between layers. Sprinkle with confectioners' sugar before serving.

Summer Homes on Oslo Fjord
Nancy Bundt/VisitNorway.com

OSLO

Although Oslo is one of the smallest capitals in Europe set at the head of a 60-mile long fjord and surrounded by forests, it is one of the fastest growing due to Norway's generous immigration policy. An abundance of land in the city used for recreation, and has enabled Oslo to be ranked very high in quality of life in several surveys. Oslo dates to around 1049 and was founded by King Harald Hardrada. This modern capital with striking buildings such as the Oslo Opera House constructed in 2008, also has links to traditional folk culture and ancient history.

The Norway Folk Museum contains 150 buildings in an open-air park that began as a collection by the King in 1882. The Viking Museum houses three carefully restored 9th century Viking longships and artifacts from the era illustrating daily life. During World War II Norway was occupied by the Germans and this story along with the resistance movement and the eventual return of the King is told well in the Norwegian Resistance Museum located in Akershus Fortress. Akershus, constructed around 1300, has never been captured but was surrendered to the Nazis.

The National Museum serves as a showcase for Norwegian artists including Edvard Munch and houses his masterpiece The Scream *that epitomizes human fears. The works of Gustav Vigeland, Norway's greatest sculptor, are displayed outdoors in Frogner Park which hosts over 1 million visitors every year.*

Norwegian Krumkake

These buttery fragile cookies melt in your mouth. You will need a krumkake iron to prepare them. Store them at room temperature and handle gently, as they break easily. Serve them plain or fill them with whipped cream. These are a favorite of my family but I don't bake them often because they are time consuming to make. Sometimes they are flavored with cardamom but I prefer them delicate, buttery and eggy.

MAKES 30 COOKIES

3	large eggs, slightly beaten		1/2 cup	all-purpose flour
1/2 cup	sugar		1/2 cup	unsalted butter, melted and cooled
1 teaspoon	vanilla			
1/8 teaspoon	salt			Confectioners' sugar

Combine the eggs, sugar, vanilla and salt in a medium bowl and beat until well blended. Add the flour and beat until smooth. Stir in the butter.

Heat a krumkake iron over medium-high heat until drops of water sizzle and bounce around when dropped onto the iron.

Drop 1 teaspoon of batter into the center of the iron and close the iron. Bake about 15 seconds and turn the iron. Continue cooking about 10 seconds. Open the iron and lift out the cookie with a thin metal spatula. Immediately roll the cookie around the cone. Gently remove when cool.

Continue cooking until batter is gone. You may need to squeeze the iron to spread the batter evenly. If the cookies fall apart, they are not cooked enough. Cookies should be a pale color.

BAKER'S TIP: After baking a few cookies, you'll be able to determine the proper heat setting on your range. I make a note of this for the next time I prepare the recipe.

These cookies are best the day they are made but will keep 2 days at room temperature. Store in an airtight container and use waxed paper between layers. Sprinkle with confectioners' sugar before serving.

Norwegian Holly
Marte Kopperud/VisitNorway.com

ROSMALING

Rosmaling is a traditional folk art that became popular in the rural areas of Norway in the eighteenth and nineteenth centuries. During this period, Baroque and Rococo styles were very popular with the upper class, and rural areas adapted these styles in their art. Strong regional styles became popular in certain areas and their names became synonomous with the area in which they were developed. Telemark and Rogaland are the most popular styles in Norway. C and S strokes reflect acanthus leaves that are dominant in Rococo and Baroque art. Flowing lines and stylized flowers are painted in vibrant and subtle colors, mainly vermilion and blues. These colors mirror the colors of the Norwegian national dress (bunad).

No rosmaling is exactly alike as each piece is painted by hand. Rosmaling is used to decorate wooden household items including small pieces such as plates, breadboards and candleholders. Chests and trunks, huge cupboards and sideboards are popular furniture items, many of which were brought to America by Norwegian immigrants in the 1800s. Rosmaling is seen today in many areas of Minnesota, Wisconsin and Iowa where it is valued for its beauty and historic significance.

Swedish Princess Cake

Almost every celebration is Sweden includes a Princess Cake. The marzipan layer is usually tinted a pale green but it can also be pink. Try placing a live pink rose on top for an elegant touch or create marzipan roses.

SERVES 8 TO 10

FILLING

1/3 cup	sugar		1 1/3 cups	whole milk
3 tablespoons	cornstarch		1 tablespoon	butter
1/8 teaspoon	salt		1 teaspoon	vanilla
2	large eggs			

SYRUP

1/2 cup	sugar		1/2 cup	water

CAKE

1 1/4 cups	all-purpose flour		3 tablespoons	unsalted butter, melted and cooled
1/2 teaspoon	baking powder			
1/4 teaspoon	salt		1/3 cup	raspberry jam
5	large eggs, room temperature		2 cups	heavy whipping cream
3/4 cup	sugar		2 tablespoon	sugar
1 teaspoon	pure vanilla		2 (7 oz) cans	marzipan
			green food coloring	

FILLING

Beat the sugar, cornstarch, salt and eggs in the bowl of a heavy-duty electric mixer with the whisk attachment 2 minutes or until thick and lemon colored.

Heat the milk over medium heat in a 2-quart saucepan until bubbles form on the sides of the pan and the milk is hot. With mixer running, slowly beat milk into the egg mixture. Pour into the pan and cook over low heat, stirring constantly, until it comes to a boil. Continue cooking 45 to 60 seconds, stirring constantly. Strain into a small bowl and stir in the butter and vanilla. Cover surface with plastic wrap. Cool to room temperature and refrigerate several hours.

SYRUP

Cook sugar and water over medium high heat until sugar is dissolved. Simmer 1 minute. Cool to room temperature or refrigerate until needed.

CAKE

Heat the oven to 350°F. Place the rack in the middle of the oven. Line the bottoms of 3 (9-inch) baking pans with parchment or waxed paper. Lightly spray liners with nonstick cooking spray or grease pans with shortening and dust with flour.

Sift the flour, baking powder and salt together.

Bergen, Norway
Hans Henrik Nybø//VisitNorway.com

Beat the eggs, sugar and vanilla in the bowl of a heavy-duty electric mixer with the whisk attachment until thick and lemon colored, about 5 minutes. Gently fold in the flour mixture, 1/3 at a time. Fold in the melted butter. Divide the batter into the prepared pans and spread evenly.

Bake 10 to 13 minutes or until lightly browned and center springs back when lightly touched. Cool 10 minutes on a wire cooling rack. Loosen the sides of the cakes from the pans and invert onto the rack. Carefully peel off paper. Turn right side up and cool completely.

Place one cake layer on a serving plate. Brush with simple syrup. Spread with jam. Top with a second layer of cake and brush with simple syrup. Spread with filling. Add the final layer and press layers together. Chill about 1 hour.

Beat the whipping cream in a large bowl using a whisk attachment until stiff peaks form. Reduce mixer to low and beat in sugar.

Spread sides with whipped cream mounding to about 2 inches high in the center of the top. Place in refrigerator while preparing marzipan.

Add 2 to 3 drops green food color to each can of marzipan and knead until evenly mixed. Combine marzipan and knead until evenly colored. Lightly dust a work surface and rolling pin with confectioners' sugar. Roll each piece to a 15-inch circle between 2 pieces of waxed paper. Gently shape over cake, trimming edges. Decorate as desired. Store in the refrigerator.

Kransekake

Kransekake is the signature cake of Norway, sweet crunchy rings baked from homemade almond paste. It is essential at weddings all over Scandinavia and a feature at many celebrations. When you serve it, start at the bottom. Slice a knife between the two bottom layers loosening the bottom layer from the cake. Gently lift the tower to the side and break pieces off the bottom layer. These cakes are often decorated with national flags.

SERVES 70 TO 75 (18 RINGS)

CAKE

18	kransekake ring pans	1 1/4 pounds	confectioners' sugar	
1 1/4 pounds	whole almonds, half blanched and half with skins	2 tablespoons	all-purpose flour	
		1/2 cup + 2 tbsp	egg whites (from 5 eggs)	

ICING

1 pound	confectioners' sugar, sifted	1 teaspoon	almond extract
1/3 cup	pasteurized eggs whites (from 3 eggs)	3 to 4	drops vinegar

CAKE

Spray nonstick kransekake ring pans with nonstick cooking spray. Dust lightly with cream of wheat or cornstarch.

Grind the almonds using a nut grinder or a hard cheese grater. Don't use a food processor or the nuts will be pasty.

Combine the ground almonds, 1 1/4 pounds confectioners' sugar and flour until well mixed. Add the egg whites and mix until a smooth pliable dough is formed. (I like to use my hands to get it evenly mixed.) This takes several minutes. Place the dough on a surface lightly coated with confectioners' sugar. Knead the dough until it is smooth, about 2 to 3 minutes. Cover and let rest 10 minutes.

Take a small piece of dough and roll out to the thickness of a finger. Fit into one kransekake ring and cut the ends diagonally so that they splice together evenly. Smooth the joint with a knife. Roll out the remaining dough until all the kransekake rings are full. It is okay to slice pieces of dough to fill the larger rings but start by using larger pieces of dough. Roll the dough to 20-inch logs for larger rings. Each smaller ring will be about 1/2 inch less.

Heat the oven to 350°F. Place the rings on cookie sheets and bake 15 to 18 minutes, until the rings are lightly browned but still slightly soft. Cool 5 minutes and remove the rings from the pans. Cool completely on wire cooling racks. (If rings stick to the pan, cool completely and loosen gently with a knife.)

Celebration of Norway's National Day in Oslo
Nancy Bundt/VisitNorway.com

NATIONAL DAY

The Constitution of Norway was signed at Eidsvoll on May 17th, 1814 and is celebrated annually.

The rings can be made ahead and frozen until needed. Loosen from the pans. cover and freeze in the pans.

ICING

Mix the confectioners' sugar, pasteurized egg whites, almond extract and vinegar in a medium bowl until smooth. Cover and refrigerate overnight.

Place rings in order by stacking from largest to smallest on the counter. Spoon the icing into a pastry bag fitted with a small round tip. Place the largest ring on a serving plate and secure with 4 dots of frosting. Pipe the frosting in a wavy zigzag pattern around the ring. Stack the rings as they are frosted allowing the icing to hold the rings together. Check often to be sure the rings are forming a straight tower. Decorate as desired.

BAKER'S TIP: This recipe makes extra almond paste dough and icing. It is possible to bake a few rings a second time if your results are uneven or cracked. You can "glue" a broken ring back together using the icing.

Practice drizzling the icing as I find that to be the hardest step. Adjust the thickness of the icing by adding more egg white to thin or more confectioners' sugar for the right consistency.

Christmas in Tivoli
Kim Wyon/VisitDenmark.com

INDEX

ACKNOWLEDGMENTS

This book is only possible because of the help and support of my family and friends who gave extra effort to help me finish. I appreciate your willingness to share recipes and traditions from your families. All your last-minute recipe testing and helpful comments make this a better book. Thank you all so much.

I also want to thank:

Joel Butkowski, photographer, who created beautiful shots and acted as art director and prop stylist.

Kimberly Colburn, my food stylist, for styling amazing shots and doing way more than usual to help me.

Beth Farrell, whose design talent and calm helped in more ways than she knows.

My agents, Gordon Warnock and Andrea Hurst, who are always working for me.

Pelican Publishing for giving me a chance to do another *Scandinavian Classic*.

Special thanks to Ingebretsen's Scandinavian Gifts and the Nordic Ware Factory Store for generously providing props for the photos.

SOURCES

Ingebretsen's Scandinavian Gifts (1-800-279-9333)
www.ingebretsens.com

Nordic Ware Factory Store (1-877-466-7342)
www.nordicware.com

Wilton Industries (1-800-794-5866)
www.wilton.com

Williams-Sonoma (1-800-541-2233)
www.williams-sonoma.com